come home.

Jesus plus nothing.

−AP

come home.

A Redemptive Roadmap from Lust Back to Christ

TITANIA PAIGE

Scripture quotations marked (AMP) are taken from the Amplified Bible, Copyright © 1954, 1958, 1962, 1964, 1965, 1987 by The Lockman Foundation. Used by permission.

Scripture quotations marked (ESV) are from the ESV® Bible (The Holy Bible, English Standard Version®), copyright © 2001 by Crossway, a publishing ministry of Good News Publishers. Used by permission. All rights reserved.

Scripture quotations marked (NASB) are taken from the New American Standard Bible® (NASB), Copyright © 1960, 1962, 1963, 1968, 1971, 1972, 1973, 1975, 1977, 1995 by The Lockman Foundation. Used by permission. www.Lockman.org

Scripture quotations marked (NLT) are taken from the Holy Bible, New Living Translation, copyright ©1996, 2004, 2015 by Tyndale House Foundation. Used by permission of Tyndale House Publishers, a Division of Tyndale House Ministries, Carol Stream, Illinois 60188. All rights reserved.

Scripture quotations marked (MSG) are taken from THE MESSAGE, copyright © 1993, 2002, 2018 by Eugene H. Peterson. Used by permission of NavPress. All rights reserved. Represented by Tyndale House Publishers, a Division of Tyndale House Ministries.

come home.
Copyright © 2020 by Titania Paige
TitaniaPaige.com

All rights reserved. No part of this publication may be reproduced, stored in a retrieval system, or transmitted in any form or by any means—electronic, mechanical, digital, photocopy, recording, or any other—except for brief quotations in printed reviews, without prior permission of the publisher.

contents

PART 1: HOMECOMING
Finding Our Way Back Home

Come Home 9
Reframe 27
Let's Go Back to the Beginning 46

PART 2: THE ROAD MAP
Following the Four-Step Purity Framework

Embrace the Purity Mindset 77
Find Purpose in Purity 98
Live the Purity Lifestyle 117
Sustain the Purity Lifestyle 139

Epilogue: Welcome Home 159

Spiritual Vulnerability Assessment 171

come home strategy guide

Introduction to the Strategy Guide 197

SECTION 1: RENOVATE YOUR THOUGHT-LIFE
Confronting the Lies that Keep Us Bound with God's Truth

Renounce the Lies and Declare God's Truth 201
    Lie One: God's Rejection 203
    Lie Two: Guilt's Condemnation 206
    Lie Three: Shame's Paralysis 209
    Lie Four: Temptation's Seduction 213

SECTION 2: RENOVATE YOUR ROUTINES
Practicing the Essential Spiritual Habits of the Purity Lifestyle

Establish the Habits of the Purity Lifestyle 221
Spending Time with God 223
Participate in Gospel Community 238
Enter an Accountability Relationship 244
Exercise Regularly 250

ROUTINES TO GET YOU STARTED
Morning Routine 254
Bedtime Routine 254
Retreat Routine 255
Reset Routine 256

Connect with Titania Paige 258
Recommended Resources 260

References 270
Acknowledgments 272

part one

HOMECOMING

Finding Our Way Back Home

1.
COME HOME

Growing up in church, I got used to hearing "wholesome," Christian testimonies. When a church member's turn came to share, he or she would politely step up to the microphone wearing a slightly more formal outfit than usual—a telltale sign that he or she would be sharing that morning—with a printed copy of a well-ordered testimony in hand. Many times these polished professions of faith conveniently emphasized the pastor's sermon and could be told during the five-minute window while the offering was collected.

These Jesus stories often invigorated my faith and filled me with hope, but at times they sounded like neat and tidy presentations with just *a touch of tension* and completely tied loose ends. If these narrated accounts had a scent, they would smell like spic and span, glossy-white kitchen counters, sterilized with a lemony fresh cleaner. (I think all of my cleaning enthusiasts can agree that that's super clean.)

Though it was never verbalized, I felt as though

there was this unspoken rule that only immaculate and refined testimonies should be shared with others. Anything that went beyond the everyday or typical temptation experience seemed too raw and offered TMI (*too much information*) for our spiritually-refined ears to hear. But as I got older and realized that life doesn't always play out like a three-act story with an exposition, rising action, and climax, I longed to know where the Christians with messy testimonies went to church.

As my own encounter with Jesus unfolded, no matter how many times I packed the details, my story just wouldn't fit into that box labeled "Offering-Time Approved Sunday Morning Testimony."

Why? you ask.

Because my story involves a sensitive, almost taboo, subject: Surrendering your sexuality to God. (Not what the church at that time would've considered a typical struggle for a Jesus-loving college gal.)

While my closest friends assumed I already knew Jesus, for years, my fear of being misunderstood kept me from sharing that I had made a genuine decision to live for Jesus through their witness. Though I'm confident that they would have reassured me that every Christ-follower knew the shame and guilt of failing to meet God's standard—no matter how squeaky clean his or her testimony may have sounded—I feared what my friends would think of me and my battle with lust.

What would happen if I shared my testimony on Sunday morning? I had a few predictions:

- The pastor would probably send out a parental advisory warning before service.

- The parents seated in the pews with their kids would cup their ears.

- Disgusted audience members would squirm in their seats with twisted looks on their unapproving faces.

- A hush so quiet would fall over the congregation that we might actually hear that infamous church mouse I learned about from my children's books growing up.

I definitely agree that we need to exercise caution when discussing sexuality. However, can you see how the lack of messy testimonies—or rather the lack of vulnerability and transparency about the difficult fight we all experience with sin— caused me to downplay and compare my salvation story with others?

Especially when it comes to lust, I believe that if we could peek at the secret struggles of fellow believers, we'd find the demand for messy testimonies is high. Yet messy testimonies that proclaim victory over sexual sin are rarely heard —even in the intimate setting of a small Bible study or a one-on-one coffee date with a mentor. Unfortunately, the intimate nature of this discussion often keeps us from speaking up to address this need.

I know this because I was that believer with a secret longing to reach out and confess my struggle with lust, but I was fearful that I'd be judged if I did. On Sunday mornings when we briefly touched on the subject of sensuality, I'd sit at the edge of my seat, waiting to hear some practical steps to help me break free from my enslaving lifestyle. However, by the end of the sermons,

I felt like a child told to build a skyscraper, given a command but no constructive instruction on how to complete the task. I knew how to "repent" by asking God for forgiveness for my sin, but I often asked myself, *How do I live out that repentance in my everyday life?*

I searched for the answer to that question in many of the same places you do: YouTube, Google, blogs, and Facebook groups. While I was able to find a virtual community of Christian women who struggled as I did and a few helpful materials along the way, some of these resources did more harm than good.

Sometimes I'd flip through book pages or scroll through support group feeds full of language that triggered more sexual thoughts. That's one of the dilemmas of those with a desire to both receive help themselves and come alongside believers struggling with lust. How do you encourage sexual integrity while not potentially contributing to the problem of lust yourself?

As someone who has stumbled over TMI in others' testimonies in the past, I know how crucial it is that everything I share with you is biblically truthful, transparent, *and* tasteful. So I gave my method of communicating my testimony a lot of thought and decided to share my story with you in a creative way. One that will hopefully have you nodding your head saying, *Yes, she understands my struggle*, while not planting any counterproductive thoughts in your mind at the same time. *Is that cool?*

If so, come with me. Let's take a few moments to use our *"i-ma-gi–na-tions."*

MY STORY

I used to walk through Lust's door quite often. With each step I took toward the door, my heartbeat accelerated, and my moral senses roared like a siren before a storm. Fantasy danced seductively before Lust's entrance, luring me in—whispering the promises of pleasure. I was drawn to the door like a moth to the flame.

Deep down, I knew that fantasy was an effort to compensate for what was beneath Lust's enchanting mask: destruction. Every time I walked through Lust's door, I became more desperate and needy. When I yielded to temptation, I got further away from who I was supposed to be.

I would often say to myself, *But this is the last time, I swear. I'll get this out of my system tonight, and then I'll be finished for good. I'll finally get serious about my relationship with God and embrace sexual purity.*

I hated it. I loved it. *Maybe I should get out of this situation?* I'd contemplate, but before I debated the matter any further, Lust would welcome me inside, greeting me like an old friend.

Lust and I go way back. Pornography on cable TV and the Internet first opened the door to my fascinations. I was young at the time, not completely sure of right and wrong, but something in me knew pornography wasn't right. My new companion, Shame, told me I should keep meetings with Lust a secret from that time on. Since then, I always looked over my shoulder and made sure the coast was clear before I knocked on Lust's door.

Lust beckoned me inside saying, "Come on in. I've

been waiting for you." Like clockwork, my good judgment would make one final petition for me to double back—to spare myself the regret, guilt, and shame. But back then all I could concentrate on was how lonely and desperate I felt in the moment.

I'd stop resisting, rationalizing that one *tiny visit with lust wouldn't hurt.* And since it would be the last time I'd be there, *I'd better live it up,* I thought. Yielding to temptation, I'd slip inside, vowing to repent and make better decisions tomorrow.

However, the next evening, I'd be right back at Lust's door.

Every time I'd solemnly pledge to do better tomorrow, but when tomorrow came, I'd find a new excuse to visit Lust again. And as the cycle continued, I wondered how much longer God would listen to tomorrow's prayer for forgiveness. *Has He already given up on tomorrow?* I'd wonder. I was tired of making empty promises, but I couldn't help myself.

WHAT ARE YOUR THOUGHTS?

Let's stop for a minute. My struggle with sexual impurity began when I began indulging in pornography. As we look at sexual impurity, you may think of a number of other possibilities: adultery, homosexuality, premarital sex, cheating within a monogamous relationship. Maybe as you read, you can relate because you identify with the enticement of lust and the feelings of shame. You've been caught in a similar unfulfilling cycle and have been filled with shame and regret from your choices. You want to escape, but you find yourself stuck.

Maybe you're feeling torn about reading this book. A part of you wants to read this book, but the other part of you feels scared that what you read will hold you accountable to a standard you've long abandoned and are not sure you want to revisit. I encourage you to keep reading, even if your feelings are uncertain at this point. This book is a book of promise and hope for you as I have been right where you are today.

I understand that sexual purity, or really sexual impurity, is not an easy thing to talk about. Believe me when I say that I understand and am right there with you. As we talk about these difficult topics, I'll reveal some more of my story, still not so easy to unveil, so that you know I am not pointing fingers of judgment but extending my hand to you to help you up rather than what often others do—push you away.

At times you may think something like this as you read: *Did she really just go there?! Yes!* And at times you might feel uncomfortable reading. That's okay. Know that I have done my best to be both direct and sensitive. I will reveal only the parts of my story that God has shown me will be helpful to you, the reader.

No matter your feelings, I'm pretty sure of this: You (or someone you love) is struggling with sexual purity. I don't think you'd be reading this book otherwise.

I'm writing this book, sharing my story along with biblical teaching, because more than being afraid to talk about it, I long for you to experience freedom from lust's grasp. I want you to experience the healing I experienced when I learned to bring my shame into the light of God's character and promise to us to not only forgive but forget we have ever been there. There is a verse in the Bible that says, "I—yes, I alone—will blot out your sins for my own sake and will never think of them again" (Isaiah 43:25, NLT). This is the real hope for us, and Isaiah saw a lot of darkness in history, much like you and I have felt and seen. So if anyone can give us some hope, he can.

But, as a first step, we have to talk about our sexuality and how we have walked out our feelings. We have to get it out in the open for it to lose its grip on us. I'm not talking about sharing with everyone. I'm talking about sharing with God and hopefully a friend, maybe someone who has the same struggle.

I'm not sure where you are with God. If you're like me, when sin has become a habitual cycle of giving in, feeling awful, then trying to change, it's hard to come to God.

But it's time for you to come home. To find that God really does care about you even as you are, struggles and doubts. I think if you understand God more, especially how much He loves you, you'll be able to come home to Him to find freedom. God, as your Creator, knows how you were created for love and how you, along with countless other people over generations, have tried to fill that need for love sexually. And His response to those before us is the same as it is to you and to me: *"Just come to me, turn to me."* Are you willing to take the first step to seek Him and His power to help you get there?

RUNNING AWAY OR COMING HOME?

I slipped out of Lust's door again. The high was over. The thrill was gone, and guilt hit me like a head-on collision. Regret weighed heavily on my heart, and the thought of coming home and returning to fellowship with God killed me. I felt so separated from Him and that certainly He wouldn't want me to share my soul with Him after I had just shared it with Lust.

I knew God was seated at a table for two, graciously waiting for me to join Him. I dreaded opening up the door and seeing Him there, waiting for me. I didn't want Him to look at me because *I knew* that *He knew* where I'd been and what I'd done. He motioned for me to come and sit, and reluctantly, I did.

But sometimes I didn't. Sometimes days, months, and even years went by without my returning back home or attempting to repent. I was afraid the next time I came home, He wouldn't be there.

So I ran away. Again and again.

What made me stop running away? What made me finally find my way back home—and stay home with my Father? That's what this book is about.

Finding my way back home took an honest answer to a very uncomfortable question. May I ask you this same uncomfortable question?

Is it possible that we trust and find satisfaction in sexual pleasure more than we trust and find satisfaction in God?

That's a big question, isn't it? Maybe you are ready to scream, *Yes, and I hate it*! Maybe the question makes you cry with remorse and regret. Maybe you're not sure what to answer. Maybe you don't want to answer. That's okay.

I had to answer this question to get to the root of

my problem. And I did want to get to the root. I was tired of the habitual cycle of sin I was in.

I had to face this fact: I turned to sexual pleasure more than I turned to God when I felt lonely, stressed-out, and hopeless. Every churchy bone in my body wanted to deny it, but that was the God's honest truth. It's not how I wanted to be, but it was who I had become: a slave to lust.

TRUSTING GOD WITH OUR SOULS AND SEXUALITY

I knew to gain freedom from the chains of lust I would have to trust God with my sexuality. What about you? Are you ready to trust God with your sexuality? What does this even mean?

It begins with acknowledging that your desires are out of alignment with God's good design for your sexuality. We initiate this journey to healthy, holy sexuality by asking God to take the desires we have for lust and to exchange them for a desire for more of Him and His soul-satisfying love. Then as we seek to live with our hearts in alignment with His will, we trust God with our emotional and sexual fulfillment and trust that He will open our eyes to see how He's created each of us to use our sexuality for good. If you decide God can be trusted with your sexuality, what exactly can He be trusted to do with it? Right about now you may be asking yourself:

What's in it for me?

Is surrendering my sexuality to God worth the discomfort?

Is living pure even possible in our sex-saturated culture?

Before I share *what God will do*, I think I'd better clarify the responsibilities on our end. You knew there would be some, right? These aren't meant to cause us shame for our actions but to put them in the proper perspective so we can see how God fits into the picture.

The question of "Can I trust God with my sexuality?" is premature if we haven't yet trusted Him with our souls. That's where the journey begins. We say out loud with our mouths that Jesus is Lord and that because of His sacrifice on the cross, the penalty of our sins has been forgiven through faith (Romans 3:21-25). We repent, meaning we "change our minds" about sin and relinquish our ambition to do things our own way. We recognize God's Word as truth and strive to live by it daily, even when others don't applaud our efforts.

God requires our complete devotion, but not in the same twisted way lust does. God is a "giver." It's when we let go of sin's broken promises that we experience the wholeness we're so desperately seeking.

When we commit to God, He fills us with His Spirit, who takes us through His redemptive process. He comforts us, heals us, gives us wisdom and strength to do the right things, and daily helps our hearts to become more like Christ's. However, God's methods of changing us many times contradict our own thinking. The ways that God softens our hearts often fail to meet our expectations, but they always accomplish God's will.

So, as a Christ-follower, you can expect God to do

a couple of things when you trust Him with your soul *and your sexuality.* God will:

- Love you unconditionally, not based on your spiritual performance.
- Forgive you when you sin.
- Change your affections toward sin and give you a desire to please Him.
- Provide a means of escape when you're tempted.
- Never leave you nor forsake you.
- Satisfy your heart's desires.

Please note that there are quite a few claims that I haven't made. No doubt, you may be reading and thinking:

> *Wait. Aren't you supposed to promise that if I wait for marriage, my sexual issues will be over?*
>
> *Aren't you going to tell me that Jesus will completely remove my same-sex attraction?*
>
> *Will I no longer have an impulse to watch porn or masturbate?*

Don't get me wrong. Jesus *can* do all of that, but I'm not going to paint with broad strokes here or try to sell you on a formulaic way to gain a fairytale ending. What *will* determine if things will work out—if giving God your sexuality is worth it to you—is your answer to this question: **If God's way doesn't turn out how you hope, will you turn away from Him? Because if your answer is "yes," then all your efforts are going to fall flat.**

If God is anything short of "everything" you hope for, trying to "fix" your sexual issues will be pointless. Being in a relationship with God is ultimately the highest good for ourselves we can ever hope for and will override all the issues we face, sexual or not.

Lust deceives us into thinking we will lose everything if we seek to please God, and I have seen that, to a degree, that's correct. We may lose relationships, quick-fixes, or addictive behaviors that keep us bound to sin, but in exchange, we gain freedom:

- Freedom from the imprisoning cycle of indulging your sexual impulses.

- Freedom from the lie that you are unforgivable and too far from God's loving grasp.

- Freedom to bask your soul in the vast sea of God's unconditional and relentless love for you—Yes, you.

- Freedom to redirect your focus and energy to living with purpose and impact right where you are, rather than where you ought to be.

- Freedom, according to God's good pleasure and timing, to fully enjoy your sexuality according to His design while lifting up that expression as worship and gratitude for God's marvelous gift of physical intimacy.

Are you willing to raise your white flag of surrender and accept this freedom that God provides on His terms? Your willingness to surrender your past sexual habits in exchange for a deeper experience of God is the key to seeing lasting change.

First, in your journey to sexual purity, you must start with a relationship with Jesus, and you must give Him full access to your soul. Think of Jesus like an interior designer. When you give Him full authority to move things around, arrange the furniture, toss some stuff out, tear down a wall here and there—you get the HGTV picture I'm painting here—that's when you'll experience unbelievable spiritual transformation. Your soul feels lighter—much like a renovation does. Only this renovation takes place in the innermost part of your being which controls every other area of your life. It can be a beautiful and redemptive makeover of your mind that helps you not just to have but *to keep* freedom from your past.

Next, you'll need some biblical and practical directions to guide you along your journey. We'll lay down a simple four-step framework for embracing sexual purity; whether single or married, virgin, or a born-again virgin like me. Born-again virgin (also known as secondary virginity) means I made the decision to lay down my sexual desires until marriage. I committed myself to not engaging my desires until I entered into union with my spouse. This is what gave me a lot of healing as I knew that I wasn't denying myself but honoring myself.

Remember, this is a framework, not a formula. We love a personal God, and He'll work with us personally. But here is what I believe is a healthy framework for you as it was for me.

THE FOUR-STEP PURITY FRAMEWORK

1. Embrace the purity mindset. Many of us trapped in a cycle of defeat believe the key to gaining freedom over sexual sin is changing our external behavior. But when this proves unfruitful, we ask ourselves, *Why can't I overcome lust?* We'll answer this pivotal question by returning to the place carnal desires began: the Garden of Eden. Together, we'll uncover the origin story of sin, discover how the good news of the gospel applies to our sexuality, and how we can rewrite the lies that we are too unforgivable, that we can't change, and that God isn't enough for us by acting on the truths found in God's word. During this first step, we lay the foundation for the journey to restored sexuality by using the A.M.O.R. acronym to commit four steps to embrace the purity mindset into our memory: 1) Admit when you're tempted and confess when you've fallen; 2) Make your relationship with Christ your first priority; 3) Operate in the Spirit; and 4) Repeat.

2. Find purpose in purity. Have you ever noticed that a lack of purity can lead to a lack of purpose? In step two, we'll discover that a "yes" to lust is a "no" to the God-given purpose and the impact God created us to have. First, we'll gain clarity on our purpose as God's creation in relationship to Our creator, God. Then we'll home in on how God has gifted you uniquely to serve others. Using scripture, we'll debunk the lies that your past can disqualify you from being used by God or that you have to be an expert to be used by God. You'll learn to let go of the fear of unfamiliar territory and how pursuing purity leads to an intentional and rewarding life.

3. Live the purity lifestyle. Good intentions are not good enough. We need a strategy for living the purity lifestyle. In this chapter, you'll first discover the sexual triggers that keep you bound by completing the 70-question Spiritual Vulnerability Assessment found after the epilogue. Using the feedback from your assessment results, you'll learn how to strengthen areas where you are spiritually vulnerable to sexual enticement. Finally, you'll become equipped to break old sinful habits by learning how to incorporate the spiritual habits of sowing into the Spirit, setting boundaries, and pursuing your calling into your daily routine.

4. Sustain the purity lifestyle. Many Christian women battling lust assume an all-or-nothing mentality concerning sexual purity, but perfection is an unrealistic expectation. By sharing about my own sexual compromises (*mentally* in my first years as a Christian and as a wife and *physically* during my engagement) and how—by God's grace—I overcame them, I invite you to see recovery as a process, not a once in a lifetime event. The chapter includes five practical actions to take when you feel like quitting and a recovery plan to put into action if you experience a relapse.

These four bold action steps create a roadmap for our journey in the pages to come, and all four are necessary to live a life that is honest, free from sexual sin, and overflowing with the right passion and purity for our lives. The life that God gives to us rather than takes from us. The life you've always imagined living—where your sexual desires and your desire to please God no longer conflict but live and work together harmoniously.

At this point, you may be absolutely sure that you want to come home to God. For some who are reading, however, you're not so sure. You think you want to, but you fear the cost of giving up your past ways. Or maybe you're unsure if this time it can really happen after trying so many times.

The journey of coming home to God is a process. Let God's love and unconditional acceptance strengthen you. No matter what our sin, we never have to clean ourselves up before coming home to Jesus. The clean-up process is His job. Giving Him our hearts is our job. Coming home to God starts by saying, *God, I don't know fully how, but I give myself to You above anything else and any other desire I have. Will You exchange my desire for my own passions for what You can offer me?* This is an honest prayer that will help you begin to walk through the door of forgiveness and healing He has for you.

Only by coming home will you experience the fullness of God's love and the identity you'll find in Him. Only in the safety of God's love can you embrace sexual purity. And it's only by removing lust's interrupters and distractors that you can take up the sacred romance

come home.

and thrilling adventure that God has in store for you. Are you ready to start? Are you ready to feel whole and pure again, or maybe even for the first time? Let's turn the page and get started.

2.
REFRAME

When you grow up a church-girl in the Bible-belt south as I did, you kind of get this sense that you know God—that He's familiar to you. This familiarity isn't the intimate, experiential knowledge that comes with years of relationship with someone. No, it's more like a shrunken down caricature of a larger-than-life concept you've been exposed to over and over again. Or like a celebrity you claim to know, but don't know personally. "Oh, God? Yes, I know Him. ... Well, I *know of Him*, but I don't *know-Him know-Him*."

Looking back, I can now see how the thought of really knowing God felt threatening to me. Drawing near to God meant drawing close to His brilliant, righteous nature, and I wasn't ready for the light of His goodness to expose the dark and dirty desires within my heart. I wasn't ready to give Him full access to every room in my soul. There were still locked doors and rooms I wanted to keep off-limits to Christ and His purifying touch.

Even though I had extended an invitation to Christ to come into my heart, it was a very restricted invitation. I distanced myself from Him, all the while struggling to maintain an impeccable religious performance—weekly church attendance, occasionally reading the Bible, praying, and paying my tithes. This masquerade was the only way I knew how to satiate my desire for a relationship with Christ and the undeniable passions I lacked the strength to let go of, one of them being a spiritually unhealthy dating relationship that I cherished and idolized.

For nearly three years, I was convinced that God had destined my then-boyfriend and me for marriage. Until that time, our story was filled with great triumphs that spanned parental disapproval, long-distances, and the common couples' squabbles galore. So when prompted to consummate our relationship physically, though I knew premarital sex wasn't a part of God's design for my sexuality, I convinced myself that it was simply a vehicle that would take us to the marriage that God ultimately wanted us to share. After all, we would not have overcome so much together without God's blessing, right?

I regularly comforted myself with such self-centered presumptions about God's will, until everything I thought I knew was turned upside down. I thought I was a Christian, but a convicting response from a friend one afternoon cleared up my misconception.

We sat Indian-style on the white, industrial tiled floor, a small gathering of leaders and volunteers planning the details for our next college ministry event. There we were, being excellent, holy students when all of a sudden—for no particular reason at all—the campus janitor made a b-line toward us. His face twisted in unprovoked anger, and all manners of profane words spewed from his mouth. I can't tell you guys what I told him in response, but by the time I finished, my friends' jaws were on the floor. In particular, I remember my friend Katie's response.

"Nee-yah!" she snapped. "We don't act like that!" Her face was bright red, and her crinkled, blond hair tossed to and fro as she shook her head in disapproval. Although she had chastised me, I felt love in her correction, and that was enough to make me consider why I had flipped out on the janitor in the first place. Unlike me, Katie and the others had modeled a loving, respectful reaction to our offender's verbal attack. This got me thinking about the other ways we not only behaved differently but lived differently.

Their faith was not a facade, but mine seemed to clock-in on Sunday mornings and clock-out as I exited the church doors. They weren't perfect, but I saw them strive to please God without selectively choosing which areas of their lives they would submit to Christ. And I wanted that.

So when I explained this to my boyfriend and invited him to walk beside me as I entered into this wild, new life of complete submission to Christ, you can imagine my surprise when he not only refused but told me plainly that he didn't even believe God existed. At this moment, the reality of how far I was from God slapped me right in the face. I remember thinking, *Why didn't I realize this until now?* To make things worse, this presented a new problem of losing the relationship altogether.

I was counting the cost of following Christ, and the price was coming out to be more than I had bargained for.

I wasn't prepared to establish a relationship with God at the expense of my relationship with my boyfriend. While I wish I could say that I surrendered and followed Christ despite this, I can't. That just wasn't my story. When forced to choose between Christ and the romantic relationship I worshipped, I opted for the relationship and slid back into the masquerade as if nothing ever happened.

CAN I TRUST GOD WITH MY SEXUALITY?

Perhaps you can relate to my younger self, knowing how to do all the religious stuff, such as going to church, reading your Bible, praying, and maybe even paying your tithes. But you may also feel bound by the tension between living according to God's design and caving into sexual temptation.

For the moment this sin feels intoxicating, but afterward, we are enveloped in guilt, shame, and regret. When we suppress our guilt by running away from Christ, we inevitably become trapped in this vicious cycle of chasing sin's high. Deep down, I don't think any of us want to be in this place, but we stay because we're unsure if surrendering ourselves to God, sexuality included, will fulfill the longings within our hearts.

In the moment, it feels like we're getting the better end of the deal when we say "yes" to lust, but I'd like to suggest that we've been fooled all along. Lust charades as a more satisfying alternative to God's biblical design for sexuality, but does lust really deliver on its promises?

May I ask you a very honest question? *What has lust done for you lately?* Because if it hasn't already...

- Made you an approval addict
- Left you with a broken heart or a broken home
- Distracted you from your purpose
- Caused you to question God's goodness
- Or shackled you to shame

...it will ultimately consume your soul. Let's not get it twisted. Lust is a "taker," not a "giver."

In 1 Peter 2:11, the apostle warns the church by saying, "Beloved, I urge you as sojourners and exiles to abstain from the passions of the flesh, which wage war against your soul" (ESV). Lust doesn't just want a little bit of you; it wants a full takeover. It wants our lives, but Christ came so that we can have life and have it more abundantly (John 10:10). While we hold back on God, lust is robbing us blind, and we may not even realize it.

We think a "yes" to lust will fill the void in our hearts, but the opposite couldn't be truer. A "yes" to lust is a "no" to the wholeness and transformation we experience in Christ and the eternal impact we were created to have.

It's time for us to mentally reframe what a "yes" to lust really is and how it looks to live the purity lifestyle.

come home.

REFRAMING OUR DEFINITION OF PURITY

I want you to forget everything you think you know about purity. Yep. I said it. I especially want you to forget any corny mental images like snow white roses, purity rings made with *pure* gold, or a woman in a long, flowing dress frolicking through some random open field. Forget the long list of don'ts:

Don't have sex.
Don't talk about sex.
Don't even think about sex!
Don't have sex with yourself.
Don't watch anyone else have sex.
Just forget sex exists until you're married!
Now make sure you only have sex with your spouse.

Are we done? Let me know if I missed one. Now let's chew on this thought. Did you know that you could keep all these so-called purity commandments and *still be impure*? Yes, my friend. You could have a black belt in virginity, maintain sexual integrity, and still fall short of living pure. Do you want to know how this madness is possible?

We've got the wrong definition of purity! Our purity is, well, not pure enough. Biblical purity goes beyond sexual expression. Our sexuality is just one piece of the bigger picture of our pureness. That's why we have to reframe our understanding of sexual purity.

The Bible defines purity as pleasing God by pursuing a righteous life. The Psalmist asks, "How can a young man keep his way pure?" and then responds, "By guarding it according to your word. With my whole heart I seek you; let me not wander from your commandments! I have stored up your word in my heart, that I might not sin against you" (Psalm 119: 9-1, ESV). In 2 Timothy 2:22, Paul encourages Timothy to "flee youthful passions and pursue righteousness, faith, love, and peace, along with those who call on the Lord from a pure heart."

Seeking God and treasuring His word in our hearts produces purity. And this may be why we're so fixated on this list of don'ts anyway. Sometimes it's a lot easier to follow a list of rules than to submit ourselves in an honest, committed relationship with the living God.

A PICTURE OF A RELATIONSHIP WITH CHRIST

What if instead of focusing on the don'ts of God's design for sex, we started pursuing God, Himself? What if we started seeing the bigger picture behind our purity instead of focusing solely on lust? That would be the beginning of an unforgettable journey to finding wholeness in Christ and ultimately our journey to true purity.

But honestly, when we've become so accustomed to the do's and don'ts of sexual purity, we may find it hard to move beyond that list of rules. It may be hard to allow ourselves to come home to God and to receive His unconditional love, especially if we're right in the middle of the struggle. In the next section we'll look at a story that I think will help you in reframing your mindset about sexual purity.

RUNAWAY

From time to time, I have a strong craving for pizza

late at night. The sun has set. I'm lying comfortably in bed, and I've already put on my sweatpants and oversized t-shirt. The last thing I want to do is leave my house, but if that craving is strong enough, I'll pick up my car keys and leave in the dead of night to satisfy it. I'll stroll right past my fridge, even though it's already packed with plenty of healthy and delicious dinner options. In that instant, hot and cheesy sausage pizza is the only thing that will do.

Lust has the same effect on us spiritually. You may be enjoying fellowship with God when suddenly something triggers a sexual craving within you. Logically, you know that God can satisfy your heart's desires and most likely has already reserved some good blessing for you. But you stroll right past prayer and the scriptures and out of God's will to satisfy your sexual appetite. You know there's healthy spiritual fruit like patience and self-control stored inside of your spiritual fridge, but in that moment only [you fill in the blank] will satisfy you.

Dissatisfaction and lust go hand-in-hand, like two love birds in a park. When we lust after something, we desperately desire what we were never designed to have. Lust distorts healthy desires for sex, along with appreciation and respect for this gift within marriage. It compels us to disregard our Gift-giver's guidelines for enjoying sex so that we may enjoy *the gift* on our own terms.

In the scriptures, I met another runaway who left home to satisfy his cravings. To me, it's one of the most beautiful pictures of God's love. Imagine you are the prodigal son. Notice how the father, representing God, reacts.

Christ's parable of the prodigal son is the story of a wayward young man who demands his inheritance from his father prematurely (Luke 15:11-32). The father agrees and divides his wealth among his sons. So with his pockets full of money and his bags all packed, the prodigal heads out to a distant land where he wastes all his riches on wild living.

> *About the time his money ran out, a great famine swept over the land, and he began to starve. He persuaded a local farmer to hire him, and the man sent him into his fields to feed the pigs. The young man became so hungry that even the pods he was feeding the pigs looked good to him. But no one gave him anything. When he finally came to his senses, he said to himself, "At home even the hired servants have food enough to spare, and here I am dying of hunger! I will go home to my father and say, 'Father, I have sinned against both heaven and you, and I am no longer worthy of being called your son. Please take me on as a hired servant.'"* (Luke 15:14-19, MSG)

What does it take to convince a prodigal to come home? Disaster? I imagine that when the son had money and things were going smoothly, any pangs he may have felt to repent and return to his Father were quickly ignored like an unwanted cell phone call. But then disaster struck. The bottom fell out of his rock star lifestyle. And, to make matters worse, a famine came on the land. This prodigal hit his lowest low before he finally came to his senses, owned up to his mistakes, and headed back to his father.

Before I surrendered my life to Christ, there were many times I silenced my convictions about my sinful lifestyle. Despite my unfaithfulness, God continued to rescue me in crisis situations, like when I was short on money for a bill, or desperately needed His favor in some circumstance. His faithfulness was like a text notification, reminding me that I was resisting Him and abusing His compassion. Can you relate?

Still, as life went seemingly well for me, I convinced myself that my sin wasn't that serious—that God would show grace to me as usual. It was only after ending my afore-mentioned relationship and having all hope of getting back together crushed, that I was able to seriously consider God's call to come home. Disaster taught me that any attempt to find wholeness outside of Christ was self-sabotage.

Have you ever considered that the calamity you experience outside of God's will might be God's loving call for you to come home? What if the depression and heartache from your last breakup was God's call? Or what about that really bad, no good, terrible day you had? Say what we will about disaster, but as in the case of the prodigal son, it'll break through to us when the sweet and common graces of God won't.

When we left off in scripture, the prodigal son was preparing his "apology" speech. He expected the hammer to fall after all the wrong he'd done. Upon his return, however, the runaway is greeted with grace—not rejection or condemnation.

> *So he returned home to his father. And while he was still a long way off, his father saw him coming. Filled with love and compassion, he ran to his son, embraced him, and kissed him. His son said to him, "Father, I have sinned against both heaven and you, and I am no longer worthy of being called your son." But his father said to the servants, "Quick! Bring the finest robe in the house and put it on him. Get a ring for his finger and sandals for his feet. And kill the calf we have been fattening. We must celebrate with a feast, for this son of mine was dead and has now returned to life. He was lost, but now he is found." So the party began. (Luke 15:20-24, MSG)*

It just doesn't make sense, does it? The father had every right to disown his son after all the prodigal had done. But instead of turning his son away, the loving father closes the distance between them. Rather than condemning his son for pursuing his own selfish desires, the father chooses to rejoice over his son's repentance with a lavish homecoming party.

Our past sin often feels like an insurmountable barricade on the road of repentance—like a great big fence keeping us from God. A fence, that despite how many times we've tried, we can't seem to climb over or break through. Whether it's secret sins that loom over us like towering walls, or big piles of failure that block the path forward, we ask ourselves: "Will forgiveness really penetrate this mess I've made and clear a path back to the Father?"

It *already* has, Sis.

Through repentance and faith in Jesus Christ, we can be sure that God has already demolished every roadblock caused by sin. It's because of Christ's sacrifice on the cross that we can boldly approach the throne of our gracious God. "There we will receive his mercy, and we will find grace to help us when we need it most" (Hebrews 4:16, NLT).

God is not waiting for us to come home so He can scold us as soon as we walk through the door. If you are ready to own up to your mistakes, if you are ready to submit to His process, if you want forgiveness for your sins—God invites you to come home.

Don't run away.

Don't hide.

Just as the compassionate father anxiously anticipated the return of the prodigal son, God anticipates your return. Still unconvinced? Look at what Jesus says in Luke 15:10: "'... I tell you, there is joy before the angels of God over one sinner who repents'" (NLT).

Where is the joy?

Before the angels of God.

Who is before the angels of God?

God.

Woah…right? I know. I'm fighting back the tears myself while I'm sitting in this Whole Foods.

Sis, God loves you. You can come home. Your

Heavenly Father is prepared to throw His own homecoming party—just for you.

Let's pick up where I left off on my story. Some months after my conversation with my boyfriend, God completely wrecked my life. As for the guy I chose over God, he broke up with me and almost immediately replaced me with another girl. The day I realized that the relationship I had made the bedrock of my needy soul was gone and never coming back was almost laughably depressing.

My clothes were soaking wet from the rain. I must have looked pitiful to even the stray cat that watched me as I cut through an empty alley to get to my apartment. As I sauntered through the adjacent empty parking lot in a heartbroken daze, I remember feeling the weight of his rejection. The unshakeable thought that I was now "damaged goods" threatened to crush and consume me. At that moment a voice within my heart, one that I could only instinctively credit to Christ, spoke gently to me:

"Nia, why are you so broken over this counterfeit love? You know that I love you, and if you invite me completely into your heart, I will show you the real thing." I don't know about you, but when you hear God speaking directly to your heart in such a personal, tender way, it's pretty much impossible to refuse Him. And so from that moment, I came home to Christ. As we venture ahead in the pages to come, I can't wait to unveil more of my story and Christ's faithfulness to accomplish abundantly more than I could have expected and hoped.

Will you answer God's call for you to repent and

restore fellowship with Him? Remember, you don't have to get yourself all cleaned up before coming to the Lord. He meets you right where you are. He'll work in you, helping you to understand the true definition of purity and even taking you to a place where that's what you long for. I don't know about you, but a homecoming party is a welcome change compared to the endless cycle of guilt, shame, and defeat of sexual sin.

DEVELOPING PRACTICAL ACTION STEPS

When I made the decision to commit myself to Christ and sexual purity, I knew it wouldn't be easy. But God's grace and mercy motivated me to persevere so that I could find satisfaction in Him alone. Every time I felt tempted to give in to sexual temptation, I did two things: I prayed, and I took the quickest escape route from temptation available. I know those don't sound like breathtakingly innovative solutions, but they get the job done.

There are some things God won't do unless we specifically ask Him to in *prayer* (James 4:2-3). Confessing your desires to God through prayer is the first step to having those desires replaced with joy and satisfaction in Him. So when I felt like engaging in sexual immorality, I dropped what I was doing and told God exactly how I felt and what I was craving. Then, I asked Him to replace that desire with a satisfaction and a longing for more of Him. Every time I did this, it was like I was reprogramming my mind to visit God instead of Lust when I felt lonely, depressed, and hopeless. But I didn't stop there.

If we want to break free from sin's grasp, we must

take action. I'm not talking about offensive tactics—pressing forward through enemy territory and fighting. On the contrary, we choose to *flee* from temptation by:

1. Running away when we encounter temptation (1 Corinthians 6:18).

2. Redirecting ourselves to an alternative action (2 Timothy 2:22).

3. Striving to avoid situations that could tempt us altogether (Matthew 26:41).

We don't try to negotiate with seduction or fight it off. We run, do a different thing, and we distance ourselves from anything that could potentially entangle us.

When I consider my own story, there was a period of time I had to distance myself from alcohol. Social drinking was almost like a platform for me at that time. The combination of spirits and the cheering of my peers just made for a very bad spectacle. To this day, I clearly remember being tackled by my friends at a party after trying to kiss my female neighbor. While the Bible permits drinking within moderation (Ephesians 5:18), I made the personal decision to abstain from drinking until my character, modesty, and integrity reached greater maturity. However, I wasn't always so diligent.

On another occasion, I failed to flee from sexual temptation. I still remember walking into the dorm lobby to play a bit of ping-pong with a friend. Seated on one of the blue, cushioned armchairs that sat at both sides of the green, segmented table, was a handsome face I had never seen before. At some point, he even joined our game. After playing a few heated rounds,

I was ready to put down the small white ball and the worn, red paddle and walk back to my apartment. I still cringe remembering how when I got up to leave, I accepted his invitation to drive me home.

Before I continue my story, let me add this point: I'm opening up about my failure here because I want you to know that there have been times I've slipped up. I want to give you the opportunity to identify where I went wrong and how I could've chosen to flee when tempted. My prayer is that you'll learn from my mistakes and exercise these fleeing tactics in your own experience. Now, back to the story.

After spending some time alone inside, the situation quickly began to spiral. Thankfully, I recovered my integrity before things went too far and politely asked him to leave. As I closed the door behind him, *Certainly,* I thought, *"I should have initially refused the guy's offer to take me home.*

Looking back on this, I do applaud my younger self for course-correcting after recognizing my offense. (After all, it's never too late to do the right thing.) I also think that sprinting away from that good-looking fellow wouldn't have been a bad idea either. This is a fleeing tactic Joseph models perfectly for us in the scriptures.

Joseph was the runt of twelve brothers and a shepherd boy. He was also his father Israel's favorite son —a well-known fact that inspired his eleven brothers to betray and sell Joseph into slavery. In Egypt, Joseph is purchased by Potiphar, an Egyptian officer, and ultimately made his personal attendant, in charge of Potiphar's entire household. It was during this time that

Potiphar's wife began aggressive efforts to seduce Joseph (Genesis 39:6-7).

Day after day, he preoccupied himself with his work and avoided Potiphar's wife as much as possible (Genesis 39:10). When she finally corners Joseph and pressures him to sleep with her, he doesn't stand there and try to reason with her. He runs away without even pausing to pick up his fallen cloak (Genesis 39:10-12).

So we see that prayer is necessary if we want God to change our heart's desires, but we must also take escape routes to evade Lust's enticing grasp. I frequently found myself in enticing scenarios, so I prayed and ran away *a lot*. Here are some scenarios you might encounter and specific ways to pray and flee from temptation.

> *God, I'm alone in my room with my laptop. I really want to watch porn right now. Instead, I'm going to put on some worship music and do some hand-lettering in my prayer journal. Please replace this desire to compromise sexually with a desire for more of You. Please strengthen me by Your presence in this moment, and comfort me through Your Spirit. Help me combat lust for what I can't have sexually by reminding me of the riches I have in You.*
>
> *I really want to take this attractive guy up on his "Netflix and chill" offer, but I know later we'll just end up crossing the line. God, it's so hard to say "no" when I feel like sexual relief is dangling itself right in front of me. At times it feels*

> *more within my grasp than Your promises. God, please remind me that my feelings aren't intelligent. Instead of giving in, I'm going to politely decline, schedule some time to hang out with my accountability partner, and trust that You know what's best for me—even though I don't feel like it.*

And that's how my prayers continued moment by moment and day by day until doing things that strengthened my desire for God felt more natural, and my cravings for sexual sin felt more unnatural. Things got tough and there were times I took steps backward, but I kept coming home. I repented and kept pursuing God instead of running away.

Now, it's your turn.

No matter how many times you mess up, God will be waiting to greet you with grace when you return.

This doesn't mean that you won't have disciplinary consequences as a result of your decisions. And it's certainly not a license to sin either. It's an invitation to receive God's love and forgiveness—even when you're covered in sin like incriminating lipstick stains on a white collared shirt.

If you're battling lust and you've been trying to clean yourself up before you repent and restore fellowship with God, you can stop trying to fix yourself. You can stop running away from God.

Come home.

The rooms inside of your soul may still be pretty jacked up. You might even want to continue visiting

Lust. Maybe you're afraid because your life is in desperate need of God's cleansing touch but fear not. God knew what He was getting into when He sat down at that table for two. Return and surrender the transforming work of your heart to Him, moment by moment and day by day. You'll always need Him, and He's not going anywhere. He'll help you reframe your understanding of sexual purity, and He'll enable you to be free of sexual immorality.

3.
LET'S GO BACK TO THE BEGINNING

As a little girl growing up in the Bible belt of west Tennessee, I spent a lot of time at church gatherings. While skipping down the aisles of old country chapels in a frilly dress and shiny, black shoes, I'd often catch snippets of what adults called "grown folks' conversation."

Peppered in these dialogues, were special phrases only adults could use like, "You better come correct." Together with my younger sister, we'd practice mimicking such phrases in secrecy. "You better come correct," we'd whisper with an attitude, snapping our fingers, rolling our necks, and stomping our feet.

While most times the phrase is a warning to approach another with respect, "You better come correct" is also a call to action to perform a task properly. It emphasizes the fact that tackling a problem in-and-of-itself isn't enough. It's how we approach the issue that can mean the difference between success or failure.

Let's Go Back to the Beginning

As a young college freshman trapped by lust in a cycle of spiritual defeat, I'd often ask myself, *Why am I constantly falling into the same sin over and over again?* For me, sexual sin was the one area of my life where I constantly found myself yielding to temptation. *If I could just get a grip on this*, I thought, *then I could consider myself a "good Christian."*

But no matter how I approached my problem, none of my efforts succeeded. I tried many things:

- If I indulged in a bad habit, I made sure I reminded myself how guilty I should feel. *After all, feeling guilty shows you're sorry, right?*

- If that didn't work, I'd create a list of rules to help me stay on track—only to spiral into a cycle of self-condemnation when I failed to keep them.

- At my peak of desperation, I confessed my struggle to my accountability partner, but since my confidant struggled just as much as I did, our partnership yielded more setbacks than victories.

There were brief times I benefited from my endeavors, but none of these restrictions or self-punishments helped me see lasting change or transformation that went beyond my outward behavior. To find real freedom from lust—freedom from my unhealthy appetite for sensuality altogether—I knew I needed a new battle strategy.

Sun Tzu, an ancient Chinese general, author of *The*

Art of War and arguably the best military strategist of all time, once said:

> *If you know the enemy and know yourself, you need not fear the result of a hundred battles. If you know yourself but not the enemy, for every victory gained you will also suffer a defeat. If you know neither the enemy nor yourself, you will succumb in every battle.*

Pretty deep, huh?

Yeah, I thought so too, but I also realized that my strategy for defeating lust was missing these critical pieces of intel (military slang for "intelligence").

I wasn't taking into account WHO I was and the true IDENTITY of my enemy. Lust isn't some 10-story tall, prehistoric sea monster we need to prevent from going on a destructive rampage. It's not an entity in-and-of-itself. It's just one of the many faces of mankind's greatest enemy, an enemy I was ill-equipped to fight alone: sin.

Okay, don't freak out. I know "sin" is a churchy word, but I'll share a down-to-earth explanation, just in case you're new to this spiritual word. Sin simply means going our own way instead of God's way. In short, "sin" is why we just can't *come correct* no matter how hard we try. Paul describes our struggle with sin like this:

> *And I know that nothing good lives in me, that is, in my sinful nature. I want to do what is right, but I can't. I want to do what is good, but I don't. I don't want*

> *to do what is wrong, but I do it anyway.*
> *(Romans 7:18-19, NLT)*

The bad news is that you and I can't defeat sin alone, but the "good news" (or "the gospel" as the Bible calls it) is that Jesus already defeated sin on our behalf. (We'll talk more about that in the paragraphs to come.)

Looking back, I now realize that I can't achieve spiritual victory over lust while having tunnel-vision for my sexual sin. **To experience transformation from the inside out, we have to tap into the power of the gospel in *every* area of our lives—not just our sexuality.**

As an unseasoned Christian, my fixation on avoiding *external* sexual sin often blinded me to the *internal* issues of sin within my heart. Scrolling through that era of my life via my Facebook feed, I can't help but cringe at the photos I posted and the comments I made. To some, it may sound too self-critical. However, when I consider how those seemingly innocent behaviors were done out of the abundance of my heart, it's clear that my sexual integrity wasn't the only area of my life desperate for my spiritual attention.

Both my choice of clothing and words needed to be introduced to the gospel, specifically through the practice of biblical modesty. Modesty is an attitude of displaying Christ in your personhood. Think of it as the *external* picture you project to others — through your words, mannerisms, and appearance— of the *internal* work Christ has done in your heart. Rather than helping others see Christ in me, my low-cut shirts and my thoughtless words more often revealed areas of my character that weren't yet fully submitted to Him.

come home.

As I began to see my battle with lust through the lens of the gospel, I discovered that God left us a winning strategy for restoring not just our sexuality, but our entire souls. That strategy is found in His word, the Bible.

Since entering the world, sin has been undefeated by man. Sin's origin story is the story of why *alone* we can never conquer our sexual temptations. To see the error in single-handedly combating sin, let's return to the beginning of lust and enticement, starting with the Fall of man in the Garden of Eden and ending with the gospel of Jesus Christ.

THE ORIGIN OF SIN AND LUST

When I first began reading the Bible, I remember it being a very rich experience for me—like a bite of a decadent chocolate cake covered in chocolate frosting. It tastes so good, but too much, too soon might ruin the experience. Friend, I want so much for you to relish every morsel of this scripture we're about to dive into and to see its relevance to your journey toward biblical purity. So to make it easier to digest, I will divide this biblical account into four bite-sized portions:

CREATION — God created everything, including ourselves and our sexuality, according to His good design.

FALL — Satan (the serpent) entices Adam and Eve to seize independence from God by rejecting His design, and as a result, sin is introduced into the human experience.

REDEMPTION — God sends Jesus to mediate the broken relationship between man and God.

RECONCILIATION — When we turn away from sin and accept Jesus as our Mediator, He enables us to live in loving relationship with God.

As we devour God's word together, I pray you'll taste and see the goodness of God's design for your sexuality, along with *every area* of your life. In doing so, you'll come to recognize that your lust issues are like rotten mouthfuls of the stomach-churning stew the Bible calls "sin."

Creation

As the author of this self-published book, I have the creative license to write whatever I please (within the limits of biblical truth, of course). Similarly, Genesis 1 reveals that God spoke everything into existence, according to His pleasure. This divine Author of the cosmos is our Creator and the source of all things—including sex. Since God has sole-ownership over all He has made, He alone has the authority to define His creation.

In His own words, God described everything He made as "good." This "good" (or *tob* in its original Greek translation) refers to something of precious value, beauty, moral goodness, and overall desirableness. In contrast, the first instance God called something "not good" is found in Genesis 2:18, when God says, "'It is not good for the man to be alone. I will make a helper who is just right for him'" (NLT). Soon Adam received his wife, Eve, who God fashioned from one of Adam's ribs. It's here in the first monogamous, marriage between man and woman that God blessed humanity, represented by this couple.

Then God gives these two unquestionably the greatest wedding gift of all time: He commands them to "be fruitful and multiply" (Genesis 1:28a). In other words, God's first commandment to this couple was *have sex.* This is because our fruitfulness within the covenant of marriage brings God glory. A covenant is what we might call a contractual agreement, *except* it's distinguished by a morally binding and mutual commitment of faithfulness to each other. The mutual *giving of ourselves* within marital sex reflects God's love for us —ultimately expressed by Christ *giving His life* for the church (Romans 7:1-6, Ephesians 5:21-33).

Together, Adam and Eve lived in paradise and experienced the bliss of an intimate relationship without one hint of shame—not only with each other but with God as well. With the exception of the Tree of the Knowledge of Good and Evil, Adam and Eve were free to enjoy the limitless pleasures found within God's perfect creation. However, where God creates beauty, Satan distorts and perverts it.

The Fall

"Put simply, the Bible defines Satan as an angelic being who fell from his position in heaven due to sin and is now completely opposed to God, doing all in his power to thwart God's purposes." (Who Is Satan, n.d.) Specifically, his plot to ruin God's purposes for our lives unfolds in his conversation with Eve, where —using the cunning serpent as a vessel— he seduces her (and Adam) into tasting the forbidden fruit (Genesis 3:1-5).

One mouth-watering bite later, the fruit's fleeting flavors leave a sour taste in the couple's mouths and a crater in their souls. The comfort and freedom they felt, naked in each other's presence, dissolves into a desperate urge to hide. They instinctively wrap their arms around their exposed bodies and sew fig leaves together to cover up their embarrassment. Their fear only intensifies as they hear God approaching and actively seeking them. Instinctively, they crouch behind forest brush, hoping to conceal themselves from their all-seeing Creator (Genesis 3:6-10).

As their actions are uncovered, God confronts Adam first. Then He turns to ask Eve, "'What is this that you have done?'" (Genesis 3:13). I can only imagine the despair she feels as the realization that she has both disobeyed and disappointed God sinks in and weighs down her soul for the very first time. With opened eyes, she realizes that *wisdom is good*, but only *when anchored in submission to her all-knowing Creator* (Proverbs 9:10). It's at this moment that Eve can see the serpent's trickery clearly. With her head hung, Eve confesses, "'The serpent deceived me and I ate'" (Genesis 3:13).

Let's stop for a moment.

Eve bought into the lie that she could find fulfillment outside of God, but what about you? Can you relate to Eve's experience of being deceived and yielding to temptation? I don't think you'd be here with me if you couldn't.

Like Eve, I too am well acquainted with the enemy's tactic of *baiting us with "seemingly good" things*, only to reveal his hidden, wicked agenda afterward. Sex is God's *good* gift of physical intimacy, designed to reflect the self-giving nature of Christ. But viewed through the distorted lens of my sin-nature, sex was not an act of giving but a means of taking. With sex as my currency, I could purchase the affections of others to secure my own sense of worth. When I yielded to enticement, sex devolved from a pure, physical illustration of Christ's sacrificial love to my corrupted means of satisfying my carnal desires.

Perhaps like Eve and myself, you've also found yourself turning aside from God's provisions for your joy and becoming distracted by a lust for what He, out of love, restricts you from having. When it comes to the fruit of disobedience, the truth is that we've all taken a bite of this futile fruit. We've experienced the negative consequences of both our own poor decisions and those of others that have impacted us.

My sexuality is just one area of my life where I've yielded to temptation. Like Eve, I know that God's design for every area of my life was carefully crafted for His glory and my highest good. Yet, the satanic influences within our culture and my own inclinations to depart from God's design entice me to doubt and disobey God.

Like Eve, I have yielded to temptation and lacked the faith to believe that God never holds back on me, even in the area of my sexuality and pleasures within that. He formed my body with the ability to receive pleasure but in the proper context—the faithful, binding, and monogamous covenant between a man and his wife. So, when I read Eve's confession, I nod my head wholeheartedly in agreement with the mother of humanity.

I *too* have been deceived by the serpent.

I *too* have tasted the forbidden fruit.

Forbidden fruit may temporarily give us a sense of sexual and emotional fulfillment, but ultimately it separates us from God—in this life and for all of eternity. When we feast on sin instead of feeding on God's good and gracious provisions for us in the right setting, we become spiritually depleted and hungry for more quick fixes.

But praise God that the story doesn't end here with sin having the final say.

Let's pick up where we left off in Genesis 3.

Redemption

After confronting their sin, God slays animals to clothe Adam and Eve, whom He continued to nurture and love despite their disobedience (Genesis 3:21). Many Bible scholars consider this act of compassion the first animal sacrifice (a ritual used to receive forgiveness for sin prior to Jesus' ministry) and believe it foreshadowed Christ's death on the cross for the sins of the world. Both of these sacrifices involve an offering of life to atone for sin because God must punish evil.

Without Christ, we are powerless to break sin's power over us and are destined to be the objects of God's wrath because of the evil we naturally love to do. Sin is like our slave master, but when we receive Jesus, He shows us mercy by redeeming us —or purchasing our freedom— and grace by crediting us with the perfectly moral life He lived.

Like the animals slain to clothe Adam and Eve, Jesus was slain to cover our sins by suffering death on a cross in our place (Romans 4:25). Three days later Jesus rose again to life, proving He was God and that He possessed all power over life and death, as well as the authority to forgive sins. Jesus is the real MVP because He became man's new representative, replacing Adam and restoring our relationship with God through His obedience.

Reconciliation

When we **repent**—that is, change our mind about departing from God's design and ask for His forgiveness—and **place our trust in Jesus Christ**, He restores our relationship with God. From that moment on, God's Spirit abides with us and empowers us to pursue His design for our lives (Acts 2:38). This includes His plans for us to live a life of purity before Him in singleness, courtship, engagement, and marriage.

When God's Spirit fills us, we're enabled to disarm and resist sin as He transforms our affections and desires into what pleases Him. Every time we reject our natural impulses and choose instead to imitate God's character, we discipline ourselves to yield to the Holy Spirit's influence over our lives.

Can I ask you a hard question?

Is it possible that you are fighting a losing battle with sin because you lack God's Holy Spirit? Perhaps like me, you've been trying to conquer sin in your own

Let's Go Back to the Beginning

power through stricter self-discipline or shaming yourself into compliance. But how successful has that been?

Sure, we may temporarily experience improvement, but when desire strikes and our resolve runs dry, we end up right back at square one. The truth is that if we could defeat sin on our own, Jesus' death would be in vain. If a better religious performance could help us overcome sexual strongholds, God wouldn't have sent His only Son to die and rise again so that we could have eternal life, would He?

If you've been fighting sin alone, I invite you to receive Christ as your Savior right now. The moment you do, God will seal you with the Holy Spirit, who will be your comforter, spiritual trainer, and source of strength throughout your walk with God (Ephesians 1:13-14). Together, you'll establish a formidable tag-team partnership against sin and grow in your love for God from the inside-out. Practically, you can do this in prayer by:

- Acknowledging that Jesus died and three days later rose to life.
- Asking Him to forgive your sins.
- And inviting Jesus to be the One who directs your heart and life.

If this reflects your heart's desire, pause to pray these things in your own words. Or, if it'd make you feel more comfortable, allow me to lead you through the prayer below.

Jesus, thank You for dying on the cross and rising again to give me new spiritual life and freedom from the bondage of sin.

come home.

> *Please forgive my sin and show me how to live according to Your good design for my life revealed in Your word. Thank You for hearing my prayer and for welcoming me into Your family. In Jesus' name I pray, Amen.*

What a gift it is to yield your heart to God's and receive the power to walk in victory in the area of your sexuality. As you learn to view your war against lust through the lens of the gospel, you'll also experience the added benefit of connecting His story to your own.

UNVEILING THE ORIGIN OF YOUR STRUGGLE

As you mature in your relationship with God and grow in your understanding of His character, you'll find that the good news of Jesus—His story—is the bedrock of your own narrative. However, God is also very personal. He cares about the intimate details of your life, and, in time, you'll see how the gospel is woven into the new life He calls you to live with Him.

So, for the remainder of our time together, I want to lead you through a time of reflection upon your journey to biblical purity with the goal of helping you connect your story to God's story of forgiveness and redemption. The prompts that follow are designed to help you examine the past and propel you to take practical steps forward toward a redeemed lifestyle (that includes your sexuality).

With a quick glance over the next pages, you'll find

that this is not a task I intended for you to tackle in the span of fifteen minutes or even an hour. Instead, this experience is divided into four sessions: creation, fall, redemption, and reconciliation. Perhaps you could work through in your quiet time with God over the next four days. Unearthing the origin of your struggle is no trivial task. Give yourself permission to slow down as you address this critical step in receiving Christ's freedom, forgiveness, and healing. Are you willing to invest a few of your mornings in quiet, engaged reflection to experience it?

Rather than envisioning this task as a mere assignment, I invite you to treat this like a personal coaching session between you and me. Retreat to the place where you do your best thinking, take your time answering each question, and meditate on each thought from scripture. (If it helps you to follow through, I'd be happy to hear your responses. Just connect with me via Instagram @PurposeinPurityPodcast when you're done.)

As you get honest with yourself and with God about your journey, I want you to know that Honesty is your friend. Sometimes being honest can feel scary, like finally acknowledging a blemish on your soul you've been trying to ignore for years. You may fear that acknowledging it will bring about what you've been dreading all along—God's rejection. But trust me, Honesty's got your back. She urges you to take off your mask and façade with God and yourself. She wants you to be truthful about where you are—not to shame or condemn you—but to ultimately lead you where you need to be—a place of surrender and authenticity with the Lover of your soul, Jesus Christ.

come home.

Transparency with God is how we thin out the thick barriers and walls that the fear of His judgment causes us to raise (1 John 4:18). Honesty helps us penetrate these walls and together, we demolish them so we can close the distance between God and ourselves. Alright, Beloved. Are you ready to tear the roof off this stronghold in your life? Let's begin!

SESSION 1: YOUR STORY IN CREATION

When applicable, use the scripture provided or refer to this chapter's content to answer.

1. Consider Adam and Eve's relationship with God before sin. How does God's word describe the security within His love that we were intended to experience in a world without sin?

   _____
   _____
   _____
   _____
   _____
   _____
   _____
   _____

2. How did God intend for us to express our

sexuality in a world untouched by sin?

> *Now the man and his wife were both naked, but they felt no shame. (Genesis 2:25, NLT)*

> *"Haven't you read the Scriptures?" Jesus replied. "They record that from the beginning 'God made them male and female.'" And he said, "This explains why a man leaves his father and mother and is joined to his wife, and the two are united into one.' Since they are no longer two but one, let no one split apart what God has joined together." (Matthew 19:4-6, NLT)*

come home.

3. In what ways have you longed for the close relationship Adam and Eve shared with God in the garden?

___

4. In what ways have you pursued the perfect intimacy shared between Adam and Eve in your life until now?

___

SESSION 2: YOUR STORY IN THE FALL

1. In Eve's case, the serpent deceived her, and she indulged in the forbidden fruit. What influences and opinions have contributed to your own mistrust or doubts concerning God's design for your life, including your sexuality?

   _____
   _____
   _____
   _____
   _____
   _____
   _____
   _____

2. How has sin distorted our identities as people created to reflect who God is? In what ways have you seen sin diminish His reflection within you?

   When the cool evening breezes were blowing, the man and his wife heard the Lord God walking about in the garden. So, they hid from the Lord God among the trees. Then the Lord God

come home.

> *called to the man, "Where are you?" He replied, "I heard you walking in the garden, so I hid. I was afraid because I was naked." (Genesis 3:8-10, NLT)*
>
> *For the sinful nature is always hostile to God. It never did obey God's laws, and it never will. (Romans 8:7, NLT)*

_____
_____
_____
_____
_____
_____
_____
_____

3. When you consider your struggle with sexual purity, what specifically comes to mind? When did this struggle become of a part of your story?

_____
_____
_____
_____
_____
_____

4. Genesis' creation account reveals that we were created to be sexual. This may come as a surprise to you if you have experienced a lot of shame around your desire for sex. However, when our sexual desires are expressed within the healthy boundaries of God's good design, it is worship and holy. How has sin perverted God's design for our sexuality? In what ways can you see sin's influence in your own sexuality?

God's will is for you to be holy, so stay away from all sexual sin. Then each of you will control his own body and live in holiness and honor— not in lustful passion like the pagans who do not know God and his ways. (1 Thessalonians 4:3-5, NLT)

_____
_____
_____
_____
_____
_____
_____
_____
_____

5. In what ways have your experiences of others' sin—whether their abandonment, neglect, or abuse— led you to seek the false fulfillment of lust?

___

SESSION 3: YOUR STORY IN REDEMPTION

1. To redeem is to purchase the freedom of a slave. How does God's word characterize our relationship with sin, prior to having a relationship with Christ (rooted in the gospel)? In what practical ways have you been enslaved to the stronghold of sexual sin?

> *Don't you realize that you become the slave of whatever you choose to obey? You can be a slave to sin, which leads to death, or you can choose to obey God, which leads to righteous living. Thank God! Once you were slaves of sin, but now*

you wholeheartedly obey this teaching we have given you. Now you are free from your slavery to sin, and you have become slaves to righteous living. (Romans 6:16-18, NLT)

_____
_____
_____
_____
_____
_____
_____
_____

2. What has God done on our behalf to restore our relationship with Him?

And all of this is a gift from God, who brought us back to himself through Christ. And God has given us this task of reconciling people to him. For God was in Christ, reconciling the world to himself, no longer counting people's sins against them. And he gave us this wonderful message of reconciliation. So, we are Christ's ambassadors; God is making his appeal through us. We speak for Christ when we plead, "Come back to God!" For God made Christ, who never sinned, to be the offering for our sin, so that we could be made right with God through Christ. (2 Corinthians 5:18-21, NLT)

_____
_____
_____
_____
_____
_____
_____

3. What was Christ's motivation behind this divine rescue?

   But God showed his great love for us by sending Christ to die for us while we were still sinners. (Romans 5:8, NLT)

   I have been crucified with Christ, and I no longer live, but Christ lives in me. The life I live in the body, I live by faith in the Son of God, who loved me and gave Himself up for me. (Galatians 2:20, NLT)

   And walk in love, just as Christ loved us and gave Himself up for us as a fragrant sacrificial offering to God. (Ephesians 5:2, NLT)

_____

_____

_____

_____

_____

_____

_____

4. What does Christ now desire from you personally? What conditions should we meet in this new covenant with Christ? (*Jesus conveniently summarizes this in the verse below.*)

> *And you must love the Lord your God with all your heart, all your soul, all your mind, and all your strength." (Mark 12:30, NLT)*

_____

_____

_____

_____

_____

come home.

SESSION 4:
YOUR STORY IN RECONCILIATION

1. Is Christ's sacrifice enough to keep you blameless and acceptable to God?

   Who dares accuse us whom God has chosen us for his own? No one—for God himself has given us right standing with himself. Who then will condemn us? No one—for Christ Jesus died for us and was raised to life for us, and he is sitting in the place of honor at God's right hand, pleading for us…No power in the sky above or in the earth below—indeed, nothing in all creation will ever be able to separate us from the love of God that is revealed in Christ Jesus our Lord. (Romans 8:33-34;39)

2. How should Jesus' sacrifice and forgiveness impact our guilt?

3. In what ways have you resisted this truth and bought into the lie that you must earn God's acceptance?

come home.

4. How is God leading you to fully experience His acceptance and love right now?

_____

_____

_____

_____

_____

_____

_____

5. Now that we've seen the big picture of the gospel and how it's been woven into your story, it's time to confront this stronghold of sexual sin from the position of victory we already have in Christ Jesus. How could confronting sexual sin from a heart fully convinced of God's total forgiveness and acceptance of you radically change the rest of your journey?

_____

_____

_____

_____

_____

A PRAYER OF SURRENDER

I hope you've found this exercise worthwhile and enlightening. Since I've been in seasons where it felt safe to take a non-confrontational approach to my sin, I know that honesty with God can feel threatening. But more than the fear of possibly being rejected by God—or should I say the impossibility of being rejected by Him—I want you to rest assured that God has already demonstrated His immeasurable love and faithfulness toward you at the cross.

"Such love has no fear, because perfect love expels all fear. If we are afraid, it is for fear of punishment, and this shows that we have not fully experienced his perfect love" (1 John 4:18, NLT). Do not fear, Beloved. God's banner over you is love (Song of Solomon 2:4).

Before our time together draws to an end, I'd like us to close with a simple prayer of surrender. Won't you join me?

> *Gracious and merciful, God. From the beginning, You created me to experience life with You—a life sustained by Your unconditional and soul-satisfying love. I confess that I'm often distracted and isolated from You because of my sin. At times my first instinct is like Adam and Eve's, to run and hide from You, because I'm afraid of Your rejection and punishment and the consequences of my actions. Would You help me surrender these fears to You, along with the stubborn habit of trying to fix my sin problems alone? Thank*

come home.

You for plainly showing us through Your word that the only way to "come correct" is by yielding to Christ and Your Holy Spirit. Perfect me in Your love and remind me that in Christ I am totally accepted and treasured by You. Empower me by Your Spirit to live in victory over my (sexual) sin and to delight in You above all else. In Jesus' name I pray, Amen.

part two

THE ROAD MAP

Following the Four-Step Purity Framework

4.
EMBRACE THE PURITY MINDSET

As a brand-new believer, the reality of Christ's presence and love was undeniable in my life, but so were the disciplinary consequences of the poor choices I'd made in the past. A part of me hoped that becoming a Christian meant I wouldn't have to face those repercussions, but in time, I learned that the Bible says, *"There is no condemnation in Christ Jesus"*(Romans 8:1) —not there are *"no consequences for bad decisions in Christ Jesus."*

Severing the first intimate, sexual relationship I had ever known felt like scrambling to reconnect my torso back to my lower body after being sawed in two. Depression swept over me like a tsunami crashes over a city, leaving everything crushed and unrecognizable.

The passionate student who lived and breathed her academics could no longer concentrate in class, so she dropped out of college. The enthusiast of all things clean and organized lived in a filthy apartment and slept on a pile of dirty clothes on her floor. This girl—whose friends always sought her out for a good time—cried herself to sleep at night.

Yes, my heart was on fire for God, *but life hurt.*

In my case, the disciplinary consequences of disregarding God's design for sexual intimacy led to a depression that created hardships for me mentally, financially, physically, and spiritually. My decline in mental health led to me dropping out of school, which disqualified me for much of my income at that time. The side effects of my birth-control caused a spike in my weight and irregularity in my reproductive health. However, the most agonizing of all these outcomes was the deep spiritual connection I continued to feel with my ex long after our breakup. (This is what many call a "soul tie.") This perpetual desire to reconcile with him and restore our relationship —though it was not an option— wore down my heart and mind. These intense feelings of rejection, betrayal, and abandonment tortured me for two excruciating years.

There were times I felt alone and deserted by God, but surprisingly those disciplinary consequences I wanted so desperately to escape were *proof* that I was His. The word tells us that God only disciplines those He loves and considers His children (Hebrews 12:6). I believe God wanted me to suffer those consequences—*not because He wanted to punish me*—but because He wanted me, His daughter, to know without a shadow of a doubt that sin is deceptive and, ultimately, dissatisfying.

Along with His loving reproof, God gave me a newfound desire to please Him through my obedience

(Ezekiel 36:26-27). That didn't mean that I no longer struggled with sexual sin. Lust never aborted its mission to entice me with pleasures outside of God's will for my life or quit plotting to ensnare me in a constant cycle of chasing its empty promises.

When God's Spirit began leading me out of lust and back to His design for my life (and sexuality), an all-out-war broke out between these two opposing natures. Daily, I was forced to choose between falling back into old sinful habits or yielding to the Spirit's guidance—*and my guess is that you struggle with this daily battle too.*

It would be some years before yielding to His Spirit became second nature to me, but initially it was incredibly challenging. In many ways, progressing in the freedom of Christ felt too *unfamiliar* and *risky*. Here's a quick metaphor to clarify what I mean when I say I was afraid to be free from the influence of sexual sin.

After serving countless years in jail, prisoners released back into society often don't know how to function outside of a prison environment. In time, some commit crimes to return to the predictability and ironically the "safety" of prison. Similarly, after God rescues the Hebrew slaves from their Egyptian captives, they murmur and complain that they would prefer to return to Egypt rather than suffer through the difficulties and changes in reaching the promised land (Numbers 14:3-4).

These stories demonstrate that freedom-living doesn't come naturally after living a life of bondage, and the same can be said for the woman fighting for freedom from enticement and sexual immorality.

In Galatians 5:1 Paul reassures us that "it is for freedom that Christ has set us free." In the midst of my depression, however, I was too fearful of the unknown to see the path to the promised land before me. Perhaps you too want to live in this freedom, but you feel emotionally or spiritually paralyzed and prone to wander back into old territory, instead of moving forward into the new life you feel God is calling you to.

How do we escape lust's grasp and learn to live free? Where does this journey to freedom begin? The Bible suggests it starts with our minds.

CHANGING OUR MINDS

> *Those who are dominated by the sinful nature **think** about sinful things, but those who are controlled by the Holy Spirit **think** about things that please the Spirit. So, letting your sinful nature control your **mind** leads to death. But letting the Spirit control your **mind** leads to life and peace. For the sinful nature is always hostile to God. It never did obey God's laws, and it never will. That's why those who are still under the control of their sinful nature can never please God. [emphasis added] (Romans 8:5-8, NLT)*

These scriptures take us under the hood of our heads to the engine that is *our mind*. On this highway called *life*, there are really only two ways for your engine to operate: with or without the limitation of a governor. A governor is a device that manufacturers use to secure to a vehicle's engine to regulate its speed. When we consider the vehicles that populate life's highway, the Christian is one who yields her engine (*her mind*) to the governor (who is *the Holy Spirit)*.

In this way, the Christian woman is controlled by the Holy Spirit, who (through His process of producing the character of Christ within her) limits her sin nature so that she can abide by God's laws. On the other hand, those without the governing of the Holy Spirit may sin without restraint.

Just as ignoring speed limits and good driver's etiquette on the highway endangers lives, when we disregard God's laws, it leads to spiritual death and possibly the collateral damage of those closest to us. But living submitted to the Holy Spirit preserves our spiritual life and brings us peace. **Only a *mind* governed by the Holy Spirit will yield a *heart* transformed by Christ.**

Did you know that when the Bible speaks of the heart, it is not only referring to your emotions but your mind and intellect as well? The "heart," or *leb* in the original Hebrew manuscript of our Bible, refers to the "'inner man' or the seat of mental functions" where all of our thoughts, desires, will, intellect, and moral activities take place (Douglas, 1987, p. 586). In their *Zondervan Illustrated Bible Dictionary*, Bible scholars J.D. Douglas and Merrill C. Tenney explain that:

> *In ancient times, as today, different parts of the body were used figuratively as the seat of different functions of the soul; and the ancient usage often differs from the modern. In expressing sympathy, we*

> *might say, "This touches my heart," where the ancients might say, "My bowels were moved for him." (1987, p. 586)*

While we typically differentiate between "the head and the heart," biblical audiences did not separate the two. (This explains why the scripture credits our hearts with many of the same functions of the mind, specifically thinking (Matthew 9:4, Mark 2:8), meditating (Psalm 77:5-6, Luke 2:19), learning spiritual principles (Isaiah 29:13), and decision-making (Proverbs 16:9) (Waltke, n.d.). Moving forward, when I refer to the "mind" (or *leb*), know that I am referring to this "center of hidden emotional-intellectual-moral activity."

The mind is like a compass producing thoughts that direct our actions, attitudes, and affections along our journey to biblical purity. Without a true north to steer us homeward to liberty in Christ, it's no wonder that our minds continue to misdirect and set us back in our progress.

The process of directing our hearts toward Christ and aligning our actions with His teaching is what I like to call **embracing the purity mindset**. Just as we input an address into a GPS to reach a physical destination, we must spiritually set the coordinates of our minds to the person of Jesus Christ. As we embrace the purity mindset together, we'll discover not only God's design for navigating this new life in Christ but a proven method for changing the way we think altogether.

Since our minds produce thoughts that inevitably shape our actions, where we choose to set our minds is where we steer the trajectory of our spiritual lives. When we open our Bibles to Romans 8:6-7, the apostle

Paul tells us that we have two options: We can choose to set our minds on rebelling against God's design for our lives (what the Bible calls "sin"), or we can choose to submit ourselves to God and His ways (obedience).

When I considered my old patterns of thinking, I knew my mind desperately needed some course-correction. I didn't want to keep circling back into past sinful patterns or continue making detours from my journey to biblical purity. However, my countless failed attempts made me feel like I was powerless to change my mind. Perhaps after falling in the area of sexual immorality so many times, you too have felt the pressure to prove that you can think and live in a more pleasing way to God. Perhaps you too feel the weight of shame from failing to meet that standard.

The bad news is: *No, we can't change our minds through our power alone.* We can't *self-help* our way out of a heart that naturally rejects coming home to God. But the good news is: *God never meant for us to take up this task alone!* We need a divine rescue from sin's grasp, and in the book of Romans, Paul gives us some insight into just that.

In Romans 12:1, Paul urges believers to present their "bodies as a living sacrifice, holy and acceptable to God" (ESV). Paul warns them that committing their lives to God isn't possible without being transformed by the "renewing of their minds." This means that believers must allow God's wisdom to inform their perspectives in life (Romans 12:2). This principle is the same one we must apply to our lives today to break free of lust's grasp on us.

come home.

EMBRACING THE PURITY MINDSET

When our thoughts and beliefs are in alignment with God's word, our actions begin to reflect the inward makeover God's truth gives our hearts. This trial and error process of matching up our behavior with our inner (renewed) thought-life is embracing the purity mindset.

But how do we do this practically?

We're going to dive into how, but first I want to share a little more of the mindset we have to embrace before we get there.

Since you and I are pursuing lasting transformation here, our long-term goal is to develop the spiritual habit of renewing our minds. This is ultimately where our decisions and behavior originate. To do this, we begin by 1) Identifying what we believe; and 2) Examining those thoughts to see if they align with God's word.

As I reflected on all the ways I struggled with lust, I've examined times in my life when enticement got the better of me, my struggle to break free from the cycle of defeat being only one of many. The more I examined these experiences, the more I recognized three lies that kept recurring:

1. "I've sinned too many times to be forgiven."
2. "I can't change."
3. "Embracing sexual purity won't satisfy the desires of my heart."

Over the next few pages, we'll look at each of these

lies that keep us bound to sexual compromise so we can learn to identify and eliminate them with scriptural truths. Then we'll end our study with my mental blueprint for successfully living out the purity lifestyle. This tool is designed to give you a compelling vision to help persevere in your pursuit of biblical purity. Let's dive in.

Lie 1: "I've sinned too many times to be forgiven."

The guilt and shame of sexual sin can leave us doubting that God will truly forgive us, making it difficult for us to forgive ourselves. When we constantly rehearse our sins and those feelings of guilt without confessing our transgressions to God, it's like allowing shame to imprison us. We assume that God couldn't possibly forgive us for repeating the same mistakes, so we cling to our guilt. Maybe it's because, deep down, we believe that by torturing ourselves, we might convince God how much we truly regret indulging in lust.

But God doesn't want us to bind ourselves to guilt. An ungodly, condemning guilt ensnares us and keeps us bound to our sin. The longer we rot in Guilt's prison, the more we believe the lie that our sin is an inseparable part of our identity, but faith in God's promise that He has overcome sin frees us up to experience His forgiveness and grace (Galatians 5:1).

So how does God's word encourage us to respond when we sin?

When we confess our sin to God, He is faithful to forgive us based on Jesus' performance—not our own. Paul says it like this in Romans 8:1-2: "So now there is no condemnation for those who belong to Christ

Jesus. And because you belong to Him, the power of the life-giving Spirit has freed you from the power of sin that leads to death" (NLT).

Because you belong to Jesus, that inner voice of condemnation has no authority over you. Instead, God's Spirit convicts you of sin, not so that He can humiliate or reject you, but so that He can cleanse you and render sin powerless to separate you from His great love. The hostile voice of condemnation says, "You're lost. God can't forgive someone like you." But the tender conviction of God's Spirit says, "I do not condemn you. Now leave your life of sin. Confess your sin, be forgiven, and receive my grace" (John 8:11).

Christ has extended us grace. He has shown us His unmerited favor and kindness, and—I know this is hard—but we must do the same for ourselves. Jesus has removed the guilt and penalty of our sin, so who can challenge God when He declares us "innocent" by bringing a charge or accusation against us? No one, including ourselves (Romans 8:33). We may not always *feel* forgiven, but as clinical psychologist and president of Authentic Intimacy, Dr. Juli Slattery puts it, "Forgiveness is a fact based on God's truth—not our feelings."

When you're tempted to believe that you've reached the limits of God's forgiveness, revisit this truth found in His love letter to us: "If we confess our sins to him, he is faithful and just to forgive us our sins and to cleanse us from all wickedness" (1 John 1:9, NLT). We can never be far enough from God to exhaust the reach of His limitless grace. So, let the chains fall, Beloved, step through the prison door, and walk victoriously into the freedom of Christ.

Lie 2: "I can't change."

When we experience a setback in pursuing restored sexuality by relapsing into old sin, we might feel like we've lost all of the progress we've made. We may even feel like we have to start this difficult journey over again or become convinced that the finish line will be impossible to cross. At my lowest points, I've felt tempted to bow out of the fight and simply believe the lie that "I can't change."

There's an element of truth to that misleading phrase. In my own strength *I can't change*, but through the work of the Holy Spirit *change is possible* (2 Corinthians 3:18). The Holy Spirit's process of transforming us spiritually (called sanctification) can be compared to how a potter shapes clay. The Holy Spirit sculpts and molds us to become more Christlike by warring against our sinful desires, convicting us of sin, and empowering us to live God-centered lives (Galatians 5:22-23). Although this is primarily the Spirit's work, we participate in the process by surrendering ourselves to Him and committing to this lifelong process.

Similar to how the clay is soft and pliable in the potter's hands, we allow the Spirit to mold our affections, thoughts, and behavior. As long as the clay is wet, it remains workable. But without water it hardens and is no longer fashionable by the potter's touch. Just as water moistens clay, God's word is spiritual water that softens our hearts and souls (Ephesians 5:26-27).

Submitting our lives to scripture helps us remain spiritually pliable so that the Spirit can shape us into vessels that fulfill God's vision and purpose for our lives (Galatians 5:16, Romans 9:20-21).

When we surrender our shape and form to the potter's hands, we're simultaneously denying our feelings and sexual desires the creative license to mold our thoughts, affections, and behavior. Paul sums this up by saying: "If through the power of the Spirit you put to death the deeds of your sinful nature, you will live" (Romans 8:13b, NLT).

So, what does this mean for us?

Since we must participate in the Spirit's remodeling of our souls, we shouldn't expect a complete transformation to happen overnight. The Holy Spirit uses God's word to teach us, convict us of sin, build us up, reveal God's beauty, and equip us for service, but this takes time (John 14:26, 1 Corinthians 2:14-16).

Some practical ways that have helped me to be shaped by the Spirit include praying God's word, meditating on it, and reading the Bible daily. Singing worship songs and Bible journaling also help me maintain a grateful attitude for all that God has already done and continually does for me. (I'll teach you how to practice spiritual habits in the "Live the Purity Lifestyle" chapter in the pages to come.)

Just as a potter patiently forms the spinning clay with his touch, the Holy Spirit will patiently work with you to fashion you into a replica of Christ. What's important is that we remain patient with ourselves and malleable throughout the process.

God will finish the masterpiece that He began in

your life. This is a promise we have from scripture (Philippians 1:6). From a human perspective, yes, this kind of life-producing change is *impossible*, but with God all things are *possible* (Matthew 19:26).

> Lie 3: "Embracing sexual purity won't satisfy the desires of my heart."

Maybe right now the desires of your heart clash with the life that God's created you for. Perhaps you're afraid that you'll regret following Jesus or that somehow, you'll miss out by denying these sexual longings that wage war within you daily. I definitely struggled with this when I felt God inviting me to enter into a relationship with Christ. I doubted whether I could really trust God to be enough for me. Maybe you're not sure if you can either.

Why is it so hard for us to surrender our souls and sexuality to God? I don't know the specifics of your situation, but one of my biggest obstacles to believing God cared about my inner longings was the result of how American culture shaped my perspective on sexuality.

Whether it's a pop song, Hollywood film, or magazine, we're constantly encouraged to satisfy our sensual cravings at all costs. Exercising self-control over our sexual impulses is equated with denying our identities or depriving ourselves of happiness. And all of this builds up into this spiritual fear of missing out. Friend, I can tell you from experience that this "if it feels good do it" philosophy sounds good, but it doesn't hold up well in everyday life.

Lust and contentment cannot coexist because to

lust is to yearn for what you can't have, instead of finding joy in what's right in front of you without it being sexual. We know that there are many parts to our lives, not just our sexual beings, but often lust hinders us from fully experiencing the life we could be reaching for. When we believe the lie that God doesn't care about our desires, we distance ourselves from Him, our Creator and the Lover our hearts truly long for. So, what does God's word say about our desires and His plans for them?

In the moment when lust seduces and entices us, it seems so promising and life-giving, right? But God's word tells us the truth about our unchecked desires. I love the way Eugene Patterson summarizes this thought. In James 1:15 he paraphrases, "Lust gets pregnant, and has a baby: sin! Sin grows up to adulthood, and becomes a real killer." Sin kills us spiritually by slaying our affections for God and hardening our hearts toward Him (Ezekiel 36:26). But when we enter a relationship with Christ, God gives us new hearts that are tender and responsive to

Him (Ezekiel 36:27). Sin won't feel welcoming or fulfilling anymore, because God's Spirit will make us sensitive to the ways we offend God.

Choosing to trust God with my soul and my sexuality was a huge first step in coming home to my Heavenly Father. One thing made moving forward less complicated for me: choosing to trust God one day at a time. I stopped worrying about the future and trusted God with each day as it came. As I continued to exercise my faith day-by-day and decision-by-decision, God was faithful to give me strength when I was weak, healing when I felt broken, and joy when life felt unpromising.

Because God met me right where I was and relieved the immediate heartbreak I felt in that season of my life, I was able to appreciate His unconditional love. Out of gratitude for that love, I embraced His purpose for my life. And I promise, sister, He longs to do the same for you. The only question is this: Will you trust Him with your soul and sexuality?

A MENTAL BLUEPRINT FOR THE PURITY MINDSET

We just exposed three lies that hinder us from pursuing biblical purity, but before we move on, I need to ask you a question: Have you been able to identify those lies in your life? It's so important that we confront these lies—and any others—to get to the root of the fears that snare us. Then we can start an honest conversation with God about the lack of trust they represent and move forward into this new life without the mental baggage these lies bring.

I've outlined some practical steps to do this using the acronym A.M.O.R., which is Spanish for "love." Think of these four calls to action as a mental blueprint designed to keep you encouraged and motivated throughout your journey. It's no magic formula, but it's helped me and members of my online community keep lust in check. Let's dive in.

***A**dmit When You're Tempted
and Confess When You've Fallen*

In chapter one, I gave you a sneak peek at this first step. Whether you're new to faith in Christ or have been walking with Christ for a while now, you'll want to begin the purity journey with repentance and sustain it by acknowledging temptation in your prayer times.

Repentance occurs either now as you begin your journey and later if or when you experience a setback. Starting out, we want to pray asking God to forgive our sexual immorality, confessing our weakness, and requesting that the Holy Spirit would empower us to resist temptation.

> *"God, I know it's not Your will that I [fill in the blank]. Please forgive me. My desire is to please You with my whole life. Please empower me by Your Spirit to quit [you fill in the blank]. Help me to consider myself dead to it and please send the resources and accountability I need to honor You with my sexuality."*

Our confidence in this prayer is reflected in our actions. We must remember that God secures our victory over lust, but we still have to battle it. And if for some reason, you fall back into sexual sin, you'll repeat this first step.

So, we repent when we fall, but how do we pray when we feel like we're going to give in?

When lust entices you, remember to pray for the strength to persevere. There'll be hard days when temptation feels irresistible. Perhaps your ex texts you about meeting up, your coworker wants to console you after a big fight with your spouse, or you get so stressed you want a quick release from your anxieties. In Luke 22:40, Jesus told His disciples, "'Pray that you may not enter into temptation.'" The same urging applies to us today. Pray for God to protect you from temptation before you encounter it and during vulnerable moments as well.

> *"God, everything inside of me wants to give in at this moment. Please help me! Instead of [fill in the blank], please help me to [alternative action]."*

It's easy to think that our actions will outweigh our prayers, but lust is a spiritual issue that we can't conquer alone. Involve God by repenting and confessing your sin in prayer to see your mind (*leb*) changed and your life and choices as victorious.

Make Your Relationship with Christ Your First Priority

We want to think and act in alignment with our desire to please God. Remember that biblical purity is about removing the things that interrupt our relationship with God, so consider your daily goal as prioritizing your relationship with Christ. How would this step enter in your daily routines? Let's run through two scenarios.

First, imagine your friends invite you to see the latest chick flick, but you're sure it has some passionate sex scenes. Do you think it would be a good idea for you to tag along? Consider Philippians 4:8: "Finally, brothers, whatever is true, whatever is honorable, whatever is just, whatever is pure, whatever is lovely, whatever is commendable, if there is any excellence, if there is anything worthy of praise, think about these things."

Whether you struggle with pornography or not, I'm pretty sure sex scenes are ruled out by that verse. So, would going to see that movie be a decision that reflected your love for Christ and His word?

For our second example, let's imagine that an attractive guy (or gal if that's your struggle) invites you to a friendly chill-out session in a secluded location—perhaps a ride in the car or Netflix at the apartment. You consider said person a great friend, but being alone could potentially open a door to sexual temptation. Do you take a chance or propose a safer alternative? Do you see how even something as *seemingly* innocent as hanging out with a friend alone—or excessive communication or availability—can create a foothold for sin? Just because something isn't bad in-and-of-itself, it doesn't mean that it's good for you (1 Corinthians 6:12).

We have to weigh our decisions, carefully discerning what will bring us closer to Christ or create a wedge between us. I encourage you to rehearse saying "no" in these situations often. This way when temptation rears its ugly head, your "no" muscle will be strong, and resisting enticing situations will stay at the forefront of your mind.

Operate in the Spirit

Making wise decisions becomes more natural when we practice living in the Spirit's influence over us. We choose to operate in the Spirit by practicing spiritual disciplines such as scripture reading, meditation on

God's word, prayer, participating in the local church, and seeking accountability on a regular basis. Think of these habits as spiritual investments that will help you increase the Holy Spirit's influence over your mind, attitude, and behavior. (Again, I'll cover this in-depth in six.)

Limiting the flesh's influence over you is just another side of the same coin. As you add godly practices into your routine, you'll also need to strip away those things that could ruin your progress. In order to determine what you need to do away with, you'll have to consider what triggers your desire to indulge in sexual sin. This could be anything from the people you hang out with, the music you listen to, or your bedtime. To see victory over sensuality, we must be mindful of what we expose ourselves to and how our routines affect us spiritually.

*R*epeat

I love the simplicity of this final step: If you mess up, start over. Repeat.

After we experience a setback or relapse into sexual sin, we tend to do one of two things: 1) We overcomplicate repentance by believing we have to torture ourselves about our mistake; or 2) We decide that since we've messed up again, we're not going to change so we might as well binge. Both conclusions funnel us right back to square one, but those days are over. In the event that you fall into sexual sin, you're not going to beat yourself up about it.

Let me be clear. I'm not saying you won't be disappointed in yourself for offending God. I'm saying that you're not going to waste time using your mistake as ammunition against yourself in practicing the purity lifestyle. Instead of letting your guilt and fear bind you, choose to trust that when you repent God will forgive you and get right back on your grind (1 John 1:9).

Walking through a season of depression was certainly not the way I expected to begin my journey to biblical purity with God, but I'm so grateful for the way it pushed me to seek a renewed mind in Christ. As you prepare to close this book and pick back up in your own journey—hopefully implementing today's teaching as you do—I want to leave you with this powerful quote from Robert S. McGee's *The Search for Significance.* Concerning the orientation of our thoughts along our journey of coming home to Christ, he writes:

> *Too often our self-image rests solely on an evaluation of our past behavior, being measured only through a memory. Day after day, year after year, we tend to build our personalities on the rubble of yesterday's personal disappointments… But nothing forces us to remain in the mold of the past. By the grace and power of God, we can change! We can persevere and overcome! No one forces us to keep shifting our feet in the muck of old failures. We can dare to accept the challenge of building a new life. (1998, p. 96)*

Let's dare to become women who dare to think differently, so that in time by the grace of God we can become women who live differently.

5.
FIND PURPOSE IN PURITY

Have you ever noticed that a lack of purity can lead to a lack of purpose?

Once upon a time, I was a high school freshman enrolled in one of the city's finest art programs. I remember when my mom took me to this swanky art supplies store on the other side of town—where one drawing pencil could run you $5. By the time we left, I had a huge artist portfolio and a tackle box full of oil pastels and other artsy materials I had never used before.

Afterward, I couldn't help but fantasize about how much I'd improve under the guidance of my new teachers and the inspiration of my classmates. In this new creative community, I'd become a distinguished artist, renowned for my masterpieces. The only thing that stood between me and my aspirations was an unexpected turn of events: I became popular with boys.

As a quirky kid who was bullied and rejected in

middle school, I had never tasted the forbidden fruit of relationships, but high school was like an open buffet. Many guys approached me—from fellow artists to athletes—and I dove headfirst into this wild, unknown world of teenage romance. Drunk on this popularity high and too invested in my boyfriends, I let art devolve from my passion into an occasional hobby.

Things went on like that until the beginning of my senior year, when I broke up with my boyfriend at the time. The relationship had lasted about two years, so I decided that I'd give myself some breathing room before jumping into the next. It was during this brief window of time that I re-dedicated myself to art and started experiencing some major success.

Despite heavy competition within my school, I won first place in a drawing competition. My instructors picked up on my newfound ambition and invited me to try out for a paid internship during the summer. I passed the audition and from there made artwork with the most talented artists within the city of Memphis.

The dream was revived.

I was doing my thing—until lust came back and distracted me again.

Looking back, I can't help but wonder how much more I would've accomplished had I not allowed lust to muck up my focus. For a split second, I saw clearly that lust sabotaged goals—not only my spiritual goals but my vocational goals as well. I shoved aside my own dreams because I was too caught up trying to make juvenile relationships last, fooling around, and repeating the same stagnant cycle over and over again.

What about you?

Has lust swayed you to place your dream on the back burner?

Or perhaps more than a dream (which can expire once you've achieved your momentary goals), you've been in search of something greater—God's purpose for your life.

Have you longed to know with confidence that who you are and what you do has eternal and divine significance? Is it possible that lust has been the dead weight holding you back from experiencing a richer and more fruitful life in Christ?

Let me be the first to confess that lust distracted me from my goals, passions, and, most importantly, my relationship with God. It would be years before I saw the connection between my purpose and my purity, but when I finally devoted myself to belonging to God, surrendering my life to Him, and embracing sexual purity, I began to live intentionally. God unveiled my calling to write and showed me how sharing my experiences and teaching the Bible could bless women with similar struggles. I found my purpose in pursuing purity. And now, Sis, it's your turn.

DO YOU KNOW WHAT YOU'RE LOOKING FOR?

Before we practice step two of our purity framework, Find Purpose in Purity, let's get clear about what we're in search of. Our goal is to find "purpose" as we live from the overflow of an intimate relationship with Christ, but what does "purpose" mean? How will we know it when we see it?

"Do you know what you're looking for?"

Find Purpose in Purity

I used to ask my husband, Gerald, the same question before I sent him to the grocery store. Before leaving, he'd confidently recite the list of my requested items back to me. Then he'd set off in his silver Toyota truck to fulfill my order at the local Kroger Grocery store. But despite his best efforts, he'd often come back with the wrong thing.

Like many people with little or no experience in the kitchen, Gerald was unfamiliar with some items from my list. So understandably, his selection would be slightly off. Like the time he bought chicken breast instead of chicken tenderloins. Then there was that time he bought frozen onions instead of fresh onions from the produce aisle. Or, the time he got tomato paste instead of tomato sauce. His selections were almost right, but they didn't meet the criteria of my recipe ingredients.

As you read these pages, I know that you must be salivating for significance and craving a calling all your own. I believe that you've been browsing the aisles of your everyday experiences in search of some soul-gratifying "purpose" to give meaning to your everyday grind. Like Gerald, you had an idea of what you were looking for—you've achieved a few things, held down a few jobs, and perhaps even earned a degree. But after you got home, you realized you picked up the wrong thing because you were never really sure what this "purpose" stuff was anyway.

I wonder if you've mistaken purpose for what you do by preoccupying yourself with achieving "The American Dream." The woman pursuing purpose from this perspective asks herself, *How can I reach my highest potential level of salary, popularity, success, self-satisfaction, and overall quality of life?* The Bible doesn't condemn personal success. However, when living our best possible lives as our most successful, comfortable, and happy selves becomes the end of our efforts, we cross into the threshold of selfish ambition. If King Solomon were to catch you in the aisle of your local grocery store eyeing the shiny, seductive wrapper of this perspective on purpose, he'd say, "Don't waste your time with that. I've been there and it's meaningless" (Ecclesiastes 5:10-20). However, climbing the ladder to success and self-glory isn't the only knock-off version of purpose available.

Another possibility is that you've been swept up in finding purpose by doing something big for God. Many Christians have been taught that purpose is found when we ask ourselves, *What should I do for God?* Fans of this posture toward purpose often consider entering full-time ministry (as a pastor or missionary, for example) as the highest means of pleasing God and ensuring that their life has some eternal significance. While I'm not minimizing the value of doing ministry (having served both on a church staff and as a missionary, myself), the Bible makes it clear that our titles do not determine the value of our service to God (Colossians 3:23-24). I love the way the Message Bible paraphrases Romans 12:1 to address this point: "Take your everyday, ordinary life—your sleeping, eating, going-to-work, and walking-around life—and place it before God as an offering."

So then, if our purpose is not found in what we do—whether it's for our benefit or God's—how do we define "purpose?" Let's get some coaching from the Bible to uncover the true purpose God has created us to experience.

"PURPOSE" DEFINED

One beautiful analogy of our relationship with our Creator is the kind of relationship found between a potter and his clay. Using this picture, Paul depicts God shaping each of us into vessels set apart for a particular use. The Potter forms a bowl for dining, He crafts a vase for décor, and He continues sculpting each of us with distinct purposes as He pleases (Romans 9:20-21). Through the lens of this Creator-creation relationship, we can also think of our "purpose" as God's will for our lives. If you've been questioning why God transformed you from a lump of clay into the work of art you've become today and what His intentions are for your life, I've got great news. While there may not be a chapter of the Bible with step-by-step instructions for choosing your vocation or career, they are many verses that spell out God's will for your life with crystal clarity.

Every command, every one of Jesus' teachings, and every exhortation penned by His disciples is His hand molding our spiritual selves into the people He's envisioned us to be. Fortunately, Jesus condenses all of God's law into one great command for us in Matthew 22:37, where He explains that loving the Lord with all of our heart, soul, and mind is at the core of His will for our lives. When we practice submission to the Holy Spirit by maintaining a pliable posture toward God's word, day-by-day we reflect the nature and character of the One who handmade us. **In relationship to this**

Potter, you are primarily meant to be His. In other words, you are meant to be in relationship with God.

However, on a practical level, a potter also creates his pieces with an ideal use or function to fulfill. Since our primary purpose is to be His, as the One who formed us, God has the authority to use each of us how He pleases. However, unlike an object without personhood, soul, or personality, God rarely commits us to one function, like a stationary object. Instead, He created us to be dynamic, multifaceted beings who achieve much and serve in a variety of roles as we grow in maturity and experience new seasons of life. Along with countless opportunities to serve Him, He also grants us free will to voluntarily make decisions about the people we will be and the actions we will decisively take.

While there will be times God specifically delegates a task or role to you, there will also be assignments He wants you—through exercising your love for Him and your spiritual discernment—to initiate yourself. King David, for example, was specifically chosen by God to become the king of Israel (1 Samuel 16:1-13). Out of his love for God, King David made plans to build Him a place of worship (2 Samuel 7). While David didn't get to build the temple himself, both his role as king and his preparations for the coming temple were noteworthy events within God's plan revealed in the Bible. **Like David, our purpose entails both the functions God created us to fulfill, along with the initiatives we pursue from the abundance of our love for God and our knowledge of His ways.** But how can we know if what we are doing is actually God's will for our lives?

Whether we're engaged in a direct calling from God or a mission we initiate ourselves, God is most concerned with *who we are* in relation to Him, rather than the specifics of what we do. Dallas Willard presents a down-to-earth metaphor to illustrate this point:

> When our children, John and Becky, were small, they were often completely in my will as they played happily in the back garden, though I had no preference that they should do the particular things they were doing there or even that they should be in the back garden instead, of playing in their rooms or having a snack in the kitchen. Generally *we are in God's will whenever we are leading the kind of life he wants for us.* And that leaves a lot of room for initiative on our part, which is essential; our individual initiatives are central to his will for us. (2012, p.13)

Of course, this isn't to say that we can disobey God and still be in His will, but rather that by being transformed by our relationship with God we can come to know instinctively through the leading of the Holy Spirit and God's word what we ought to do in any given situation (Piper, 2018).

Paul says it like this in Romans 12:1-2:

come home.

> *And so, dear brothers and sisters, I plead with you to give your bodies to God because of all he has done for you. Let them be a living and holy sacrifice—the kind he will find acceptable. This is truly the way to worship him. Don't copy the behavior and customs of this world, but let God transform you into a new person by changing the way you think. Then you will learn to know God's will for you, which is good and pleasing and perfect. (NLT)*

As we walk in the newness of God's renovation of our souls, we come to understand what His will is for us. This is encouraging because the Bible is essentially saying that we don't always have to receive "a sign" or some special revelation from God in order to jump on an opportunity already affirmed in scripture. While God may direct us to our callings (through a dream, a conversation, our thoughts, or another believer, for example), scripture suggests that it's more natural for us to discern God's will for ourselves as we grow in our love for and knowledge of Him (Philippians 1:9-11).

These guidelines outlined in God's word have been great references and aids to my own understanding of God's will for my life. Specifically, my experience of God calling me to write comes to mind. I'd love to share a little of my story to give you a bit of practical insight into how this may translate from the pages of scripture into everyday life.

Some countless afternoon shifts into my daily routine at the office, God impressed upon my heart the thought of beginning a blog for Christian women. Since I had never previously considered myself a writer or felt qualified to pursue it, this possibility felt alien to me. However, the persistence of this thought drove me to pray diligently to discern if it could be God's leading before taking any further action.

First, I consulted my husband and asked him to confirm this with God. (Knowing that God chose my husband to be the leader of our household, I knew I could trust God to reveal this calling to Gerald if it was truly His will.) After Gerald felt certain that God was communicating the same to him, we approached our elders at our church for their insight, blessing, and guidance on moving forward. Their emphatic, positive response gave us the final bit of encouragement we needed to move forward. However, there were loved ones who opposed the idea because of financial concerns. While my husband and I didn't let that discourage us, we too were concerned about how I could bring in income, so I brought this concern to God in prayer:

> *God, You know that I've been a missionary before and how I hated fundraising to support myself. Now that I am married, I have a family. I cannot abandon the shared burden of our finances by quitting my job without a means of supporting us financially. That would not be loving to my husband or in alignment with Your word (1 Timothy 5:8). If this is where You are directing me, please pro-*

vide a way to meet my family's financial needs. In Jesus' name, Amen.

Two weeks later, my husband received a job offer that equaled a combination of both of our salaries at the time, eliminating our financial barrier and freeing me to pursue Christian writing fulltime. I still remember jumping, shouting, and running for joy around our cramped one-bedroom apartment that afternoon. Looking into each other's eyes, my husband and I could see the mutual amazement at how God had moved and made His leading so evident to us.

After reading about my experience, it's possible that you feel hopeful about your own, but it's equally possible that you may feel a bit discouraged. Perhaps you're questioning why your own process of discernment hasn't run as smoothly as the one I just described. Let me begin by saying this is one rare, isolated instance in my life where God's leading was obvious, and everything fell quickly into place or me. Other attempts at discerning my purpose, especially as I've adopted a new pace of life as a mom, haven't been as easy to navigate.

Whether you feel God directing you to a specific purpose in this season of your life or not, in both cases, you'll need to walk through your own process of discerning your calling so that you can craft and execute an action plan in response.

DISCERN YOUR PURPOSE

While the rest of the city sleeps, Kaale and his companions take to the backstreets of Mumbai, India, with a miner's pan and a brush. In the filthy alleys of the jewelry making district, they crouch low to the pavement, sweeping up fallen dust and debris from small-time goldsmiths who bathed there earlier in secret. Kaale gathers the dust indiscriminately, even sweeping dog dung into his pile. Then, he carefully places it in his old gold miner's pan to sift through the trash for hidden treasure.

First, Kaale uses a bit of water to suspend the rubbish. Next, he swirls the pan so that the tiny specks of gold settle at the bottom, while the unwanted bits of trash float along the water's surface for him to remove. He passes some time cautiously stirring and shaking the pan, allowing the excess dirt to wash off of the mixture until the hidden particles of gold emerge from beneath.

I imagine that at first glance, the average passerby would never guess that you could mine gold from a back alley. But with a little ingenuity and a process to distinguish the trash from the golden flakes inside, Kaale regularly produces gold nuggets to resell. To outsiders, the abandoned streets may look like a dump, but Kaale and his friends see its potential to be a gold mine.

Perhaps, like Kaale, you can see the potential for a rich, rewarding calling right where God has you. Or maybe this season of your life feels more like a smelly back alley. Wherever you are, the good news is that if we apply God's pattern for discernment in our lives, we too can sift through everyday distractions and enticements to uncover the potential for a purpose-driven life. Let's consider some biblical principles along with this image of gold panning to consider how we might discern if a potential assignment or initiative is within God's will.

- **Sift it through the word of God.** Since the Bible is the infallible source of wisdom concerning God's will, the scriptures are where this process of discerning our purpose begins. God's Spirit will never lead us to do anything that conflicts with His word. Even our spiritual gifts (such as prophecy) are subject to and must be tested by scripture. (1 Corinthians 14:37-38). The apostle Paul even goes so far as to say that our love for God should abound with the knowledge of Him. If our love isn't informed by the truth of who He is and His desires for our lives, then our choices won't produce His morally perfect character within us (Romans 10:1-3).

- **Shake and stir it with prayer and fasting.** Through prayer, we can ask God for the wisdom to discern the difference between a good thing to do and the right thing to do in our unique circumstance. Another way God gives us spiritual clarity is through the spiritual habit of fasting. (If you are unfamiliar with fasting, it is a committed period of abstaining from something essential or comforting to you, such as food or social media, in order to build intimacy with God. In this case, when you begin to experience cravings for what's been laid down, you can turn to God in prayer, requesting clarity about this potential mission.

- **Have it appraised by mature believers.** Just as Kaale must have his gold appraised by a jeweler before it is bought, it is wise for believers to share their potential vocational or missional pursuits with mature Christians who can give us potential insights or constructive criticism. Present this potential venture to a Christian who knows you well enough to tell you if it would be a healthy and godly decision for you. God can use this individual (or individuals) to clarify and encourage your next steps, or in some cases, to save you from acting prematurely.

Once you feel confident that you've heard from God or that your initiative is affirmed in scripture and yields to the pace and season you're currently in, then you're free to take your purpose from the planning phase to execution! The guidelines I've prepared for crafting an action plan to execute your purpose are no magical, concrete formula for living out your purpose. What's most important is a posture of obedience wherever God is calling us. However, the questions and prompts we'll walk through do facilitate an insightful and tailored experience in discovering how finding purpose in purity could look in your life. Let's get started.

come home.

CRAFT YOUR ACTION PLAN

Now that we've come to the *Craft Your Action Plan* portion of the chapter, I'll assume that you either: 1) feel God is directing you to a specific calling; or 2) desire some practical exercises to help you initiate some service to God yourself. Regardless of where you are, the following activities are designed to help you solidify your goals so that you can take intentional, consistent action along your journey. Now without further ado, here are three practical steps for homing in on your purpose:

Step One: Reflect on Your Story

First, you'll reflect on your personal story to identify themes and motifs in your life. Consider your past experiences and journal through the following questions to better understand how you're bent.

- What events and people have influenced you the most?

- What recurring activities, situations, interests, and/or people groups do you recognize?

- Until this point, which jobs have energized you?

- Which jobs left you feeling drained?

You can also gain additional insight into your personality and spiritual gifts by serving in your local church. Through your experience serving and the affirmation of members and leaders invested in you, you'll come to know more of your personality and giftings for yourself. Of course, there are personality assessments you could take as well (such as the Myers-Briggs test or the Enneagram test). While they may offer some people additional insights about their personality qualities, I've found that my test results or my knowing my "type" has never progressed beyond having conversations with others about what "type" they are. However, my experiences serving within and participating in the church have become the basis of the ministry I do today.

Step Two: Find the Problem You Want to Help Solve

Next, it's time to ask yourself, "What's the problem I want to help solve?" Passion is great and all, but you'll need commitment and hard work to breathe life into your vision. If all your living expenses were covered, would you do this thing for free? If someone brought it up in conversation, would you spend hours talking or learning about it? Can you see yourself doing this thing for years to come? If you've answered "yes" to this question, you might've found your sweet spot, Sis.

Step Three: Become a Part of the Solution

For many of us, finding our thing will take a little longer than the span of reading this chapter and working through its exercises. And that's okay. Take your time. Once you've *found your thing*, next, it'll be time to *do your thing* by becoming a part of your problem's solution. Assess where you currently are in relation to your goal. Do you already possess the skills to make this happen, or will you need to learn them? Are you a part of any communities related to it? Will you need to purchase any essential items to participate?

For now, list three actions you can take to pursue this calling. ***Go ahead and write down your first three goals below.***

GOAL #1

_____
_____
_____
_____

GOAL #2

_____
_____
_____
_____

GOAL #3

_____
_____
_____
_____

Find Purpose in Purity

After you're satisfied with the responses from this exercise, you'll incorporate the goals you recorded above, along with consistent spiritual disciplines, into your weekly routine to construct your ideal purity lifestyle (the focus of the next chapter). I highly recommend swapping out old habits that trigger sexual sin with these new ones that advance your personal goals. Casting vision over this time that you're intentionally seeking the Lord will help you persevere in pursuing purity, which is the fourth and final step of our four-step framework.

As our time together draws to an end, I want to acknowledge that pursuing your purpose may take you outside of your comfort zone. But fear doesn't have to have the last say, because God has not given you a Spirit of fear but of power, love, and self-discipline (2 Timothy 1:7).

Now, as you proceed to the third step of our purity framework, Live the Purity Lifestyle, be of great courage! While you may at times feel besieged by the lies that you're too far gone or that you don't measure up, praise God that in Christ, you've been prequalified to live a life of purpose. Rather than disqualify you, your failures uniquely position you to minister in ways other believers may not possess the equipping to serve. You don't have to worry IF God will use you—He has already begun a great work in you and promises to bring it to completion (Philippians 1:6).

Today, you have choices. You can choose to no longer allow lust to distract you. You can choose to no longer let your past sin resign you to passivity. You can choose to pioneer the course for those behind you—to

come home.

forge a new legacy of godliness. Allow yourself to anticipate all that God will do through you as you surrender yourself to His will, His ways, and His purposes.

6.
LIVE THE PURITY LIFESTYLE

I'm crazy about my part-time gig teaching children English online. To my surprise, I fell in love with signing in online in the wee hours of my weekend mornings, wearing a smile on my face and a monkey puppet on one hand. Seeing each young child's eyes light up when they learn how to describe the weather and earn a virtual reward of a paper scoop of ice cream just makes my day.

While most of my students favor the latter half of our lesson when we play games that help them apply their new vocabulary and sentences, the foundation of the day's learning begins with the first half of our teaching when they are introduced to new words and grammatical concepts. I know that the sense of accomplishment these five-year-olds get when they complete a task feels rewarding but executing their knowledge wouldn't be possible without receiving that initial instruction.

come home.

Perhaps like these enthusiastic young learners, you too are more excited by acting on what you've learned rather than the learning process itself. If so, I've got good news for you: Now that we've worked through the initial foundational concepts of our journey to restored sexuality (the first two steps of our 4-Step Framework for Embracing Purity), it's time to engage and apply these transformational principles in our everyday routines by first creating a custom strategy for living out the purity lifestyle.

Let me be the first to confess that "strategy" has never been my favorite part of brainstorming my goals. Why? Because strategy requires discipline. As I look back on the times I've lacked intentionality in my planning and discipline in my action, I can see that when I failed to strategize, I fell into these goal-setting traps:

- Instead of taking immediate action, I procrastinated by dreaming about action I planned to take in the future—when it would feel comfortable and convenient—but without accountability or a time-bound goal, "later" never came.

- Because denying my desires made me feel restricted, I lacked the willpower to exercise the discipline necessary to achieve my strategy.

- Rather than being led by my values and vision, I was led by the unpredictability and urgency of my feelings, so my efforts were always inconsistent.

If you think that having a strategy sounds intimidating or boring, you're not alone. I too thought that strategizing felt rigid and, initially, too time consuming. But when I compared my fruitless efforts with the potential progress I could see from consistent, intentional efforts, I accepted that strategy wasn't optional if I wanted a breakthrough because:

- Strategy empowers me to act right now by giving me a practical plan to achieve my goal and measure my progress, enabling me to see how each small step advances me to the finish line.

- Strategy is the gym that strengthens my willpower so I can exercise discipline and commit to showing up every day.

- Strategy propels me by becoming the vehicle that transports me from where I am now to where I want to be as a person.

Do you see the pivotal role that strategy plays in our journey to surrendering our souls and sexuality to God? When we fail to employ a strategy to create and sustain this new, biblically pure lifestyle, we resign ourselves to an endless cycle of wasted effort instead of realizing the freedom and transformation we envision. I think we can all agree that *ain't nobody got time for that*, sis. So let's get strategizing.

But before we dive into that, let's take a moment to celebrate your progress. Seriously, girlfriend! You've made it to chapter six of what has hopefully been a very relatable, but challenging read. I don't think it's

come home.

dramatic to say this is worthy of pausing to praise God for the steps you've taken forward up until this point:

> *Lord, thank You for Your faithfulness. The enemy wants this beautiful one to doubt and to mistakenly think that her efforts so far are insignificant. But we know that every action she's taken thus far pleases You immensely and greatly honors You. Holy Spirit, please continue to support her with Your strength and encouragement and remind her that she is never alone. We know this pursuit of restored sexuality isn't quite over yet, but we thank You for loving us completely right where we are and for the confident hope that You will continue to walk with us in the days to come. In Jesus' name, Amen.*

Alright, sis, back to applying the fundamental concepts of biblical purity by creating your custom strategy.

CREATING YOUR CUSTOM STRATEGY

Before I explain the next steps for creating your strategy for living the purity lifestyle, I want to briefly revisit a crucial point from chapter three. Remember that pretty epic quote about strategizing from Chinese military strategist Sun Tzu? While it's not a Bible verse, there's certainly truth in this quote worth applying to this conversation. Let's take another look at this ancient wisdom:

> *If you know the enemy and know yourself, you need not fear the result of a hundred battles. If you know yourself but not the enemy, for every victory gained you will also suffer a defeat. If you know neither the enemy nor yourself, you will succumb in every battle.* (Sun Tzu, 2019, p. 40)

While Sun Tzu's speaks to physical warfare, his words can definitely be applied to our spiritual battle against lust. Knowing our enemies and ourselves is vital to gaining victory over the temptations that entice us to wave our white flags in surrender to ensnaring carnal pleasures.

Who are our enemies? The Bible warns us that the world (meaning the man-made systems and attitudes that govern the Earth) is opposed to Christ-followers and that our enemy, Satan, prowls around like a roaring lion seeking to destroy the spiritually complacent (1 Peter 5:8). Since even our hearts are compromised by the deceitfulness of sin, it's critical that we recognize the attitudes, thoughts, and behaviors we harbor that become stumbling blocks to living as women who have experienced God's restoration in our lives, including the area of sexuality.

To know both the enemy and ourselves, we'll begin crafting a tailored strategy for living the purity lifestyle by completing the Spiritual Vulnerability Assessment found after the epilogue. Based on your assessment results, you'll be provided with practical guidance on fortifying areas where you are vulnerable to sexual sin.

After becoming familiar with both our opposition and ourselves, this intelligence will inform the way we engage the enemy in the battles ahead. To this end, you'll craft your own defensive responses to the enemy's attacks based on your assessment results. Finally, you'll learn new spiritual habits to incorporate into your daily routines. (Think of them as offensive tactics that keep lust from gaining a foothold in your life.)

Are you ready to start winning the battle against lust with your own personalized strategy? **Begin by taking the Spiritual Vulnerability Assessment, review your results, and then rendezvous with me in the section below.**

REFLECTING ON YOUR RESULTS

Most people believe that wisdom comes from experience, but American educator John Dewey argued that it isn't our experiences but rather *reflecting* on our experiences that make us wise. In other words, we gain insight when we contemplate and learn from our experiences. Now that you've discovered areas where you are vulnerable to lust and several ways to defend yourself, it's time to reflect on your results to gain insight concerning your next steps in this journey.

Let's begin processing your results by identifying your top three areas of vulnerability. Since these are go-to openings where enticement has been able to slip in and disrupt your progress in embracing biblical purity, they are compromised areas that urgently need to be reinforced with disciplined action. Once you have singled out your top three vulnerabilities, take a moment to process your next steps by answering the reflection questions below for each opening:

- What has led you to become vulnerable in this area? Ask yourself, "What need am I trying to meet through this habit, and why don't I trust God to meet this need on my behalf?"

- What are the habits I practice regularly that contribute to this specific vulnerability? (*We will discuss some mind shifts and healthy alternatives to replace these bad habits within the following section.*)

- How is God's Spirit convicting you to break these habits? What is the first initial step of obedience you can take to overcome this spiritual stumbling block?

- Who can firmly, but lovingly, hold me accountable for taking this first step?

Did you take your time to think carefully and honestly about the questions above? Your thoughtful responses are critical to the initial phase of your strategy. If you're ready to move on, let's dive into the next phase of creating your custom strategy: replacing bad habits with new spiritual habits that lead to wholeness in Christ.

come home.

THREE SPIRITUAL HABITS OF THE PURITY LIFESTYLE

Through taking the Spiritual Vulnerability Assessment and reflecting on its results, we came to know both ourselves and our enemy better as it relates to our goal of experiencing restored sexuality through the transformation that comes through knowing Christ. First, your assessment results revealed areas where you're vulnerable to lust's attacks. These vulnerabilities encompass personal habits—such as watching a particular show or spending time with a particular person—that reinforce your desire to indulge in sexual immoral activities. Then, you reflected on these results to decide your next steps. Now that we've gained clarity concerning these two elements, we can begin eliminating our opposition, specifically the bad habits or vulnerabilities that expose us to lust's attacks.

But let's be realistic about this: Breaking bad habits isn't easy. It would be unwise for me to simply say, "Alright, now stop doing all those bad things" without some plan to help us transition into the new habits and routines we desire to form. So how can we rid ourselves of these harmful behaviors?

We break old habits by replacing them with new, healthier habits. In this case, you'll want to take the time and effort you've exerted on your vulnerabilities and instead devote them to practicing spiritual habits, such as Bible study, that will help you love and desire God more. In this way, you'll create your own strategy for living the purity lifestyle.

As I introduce these spiritual habits, please remember that the Holy Spirit is the catalyst for change in your heart. Yes, strategy is important to help you stay focused and intentional, but change is made in the strength the Spirit supplies us (Ephesians 3:14-19). Your soul is not an object or project you can revamp with some magic formula, so try not to fall into the trap of relying on behavior modification to "fix" you. Remember, change comes about by growing in your relationship with God and allowing His Spirit to mold your heart through obedience and worship.

Spiritual Habit #1: Sow into the Spirit

I took in the scent of fragrant flowers, the sound of buzzing bees, and the vibrant sight of hundreds of plant varieties—some familiar and some so beautiful and bizarre I could spend hours in awe of their splendid silhouettes and captivating colors. That first experience at a local plant nursery inspired me to try out gardening for myself. In the back of my mother's yard, I sowed seeds of vegetables, fruit, and herbs for tea. Some months later, the seeds I scattered and planted carefully in the soil bore a bounty of delicious crops, which I used in homemade dishes like fried green tomatoes.

My garden was able to flourish because I took the time to cultivate it by sowing seeds into the soil, watering them consistently, being careful to expose them to enough sun, and removing any weeds that could choke them or steal the nutrients meant for their growth. In due time, I was able to reap my personal harvest of delectable produce because of these efforts. Similarly, if we expect to reap a harvest of biblical purity, we must commit to cultivating a lifestyle of righteous living, what the Bible calls "sowing into the Spirit."

As we open our Bibles to Galatians 6:8, we see that Paul uses gardening imagery to break down this spiritual habit, with our habits being the seeds and the soil being either our flesh or our spirit. Paul writes, "For the one who sows to his flesh [his sinful capacity, his worldliness, his disgraceful impulses] will reap from the flesh ruin and destruction, but the one who sows to the Spirit will from the Spirit reap eternal life" (AMP). John defines "eternal life" in John 17:3 as knowing God in a close, relational way.

Sowing into the Spirit also produces the fruit of love, joy, peace, patience, kindness, goodness, faithfulness, gentleness, and self-control within us (Galatians 5:22-23). Our every good habit, decision, and exercise of self-control is an investment in the Holy Spirit's influence over our lives. The more we invest, the greater the harvest of holiness we'll reap within our lives.

But what seeds should we sow?

What are some practical ways we can invest into the Spirit? (Note: While I'll briefly summarize four spiritual disciplines below, there's a beginner's guide with more detailed instruction located in the Come Home Strategy Guide.)

Spend Time with God

The highest fruit-yielding seed in our spiritual garden is the discipline of spending time with God. Perhaps this is new to you, or perhaps like me, you've struggled with pressing pause to be still in His presence. Why is the most productive discipline often the most difficult to carry out? Jennie Allen, author of *Get Out of Your Head*, writes, "Because real, connected, intimate time with Jesus is the very thing that grows our faith, shifts our minds, brings about revival in our souls, and compels us to share Jesus with others. …To put it plainly: all hell is against us meeting with Jesus" (2020, p. 70).

Spending time with God doesn't have to be intimidating or complicated. Here's a simple routine to help you get started. Begin with a short prayer of thanks. Ask God to help you understand what you read that morning. Using a Bible reading plan, select a passage to reflect on. Take your time observing the scripture and journal any applicable points you notice. Afterward, pray, asking God to reveal ways you can apply what you learn to your life. You can also confess any sin you're struggling with or worries you have and make requests.

Participate in Gospel Community

When I planned out my garden space, specifically where I would grow each type of plant and what would grow beside it, I implemented a gardening strategy called "companion planting." Expert gardeners recommended that you plant mutually beneficial plants, such as basil, oregano, and parsley, next to each other to produce better quality crops and higher yields. More benefits of these plant-partnerships include pest control, soil fertility, natural trellising, shade regulation, and weed control. (What is companion, n.d.)

Like plants, Christians grow best and yield more fruit when we're together. As a Christ-follower, you're a member of the church, who the Bible calls the body of Christ. This global body of believers is expressed locally in "churches," or groups of believers who meet regularly for worship, Bible teaching, and service. We participate in gospel community through membership in a local church. You could say that like companion plants, being in fellowship with believers of different walks of life, ages, and maturity levels offers the benefits of spiritual:

- Pest control: Church family and leaders provide protection from isolation and the influence of false teachers.

- Soil fertility: Biblical teaching and accountability condition the soil of our hearts to produce good fruit.

- Natural trellising: The mutual building up of character between believers is like the scaffolding one plant provides to a climbing plant.

- Shade regulation: The loving provision and tangible service of fellow believers refreshes us and keeps us from being scorched by the sun.

- Weed control: In the context of gospel community where you are known and biblical standards are taken seriously, you are conditioned to resist and reject the weeds of sinful strongholds (such as sexual immorality), and they are less likely to flourish.

Enter an Accountability Relationship

Think of this spiritual discipline as an extension of our previous seed, *Participate in Gospel Community*. The Bible encourages Christians to both confess their sin and restore believers caught in habitual patterns of sin. King Solomon writes in Ecclesiastes 4:9-10, "Two people are better off than one, for they can help each other succeed. If one person falls, the other can reach out and help. But someone who falls alone is in real trouble" (NLT). So how do we engage in accountability relationships as we pursue purity?

Prayerfully ask another believer to come alongside you by holding you accountable to God's word. To prevent your accountability relationship from spiraling into sin, choose someone of the same sex as you, who doesn't share your struggle. (If you wrestle with same-sex attraction, *confide in a woman you don't find attractive*.) Once you've decided who to approach, reach out to them to see if you can meet and discuss the matter privately. You may say something like: "[Person's name], I consider you a great role model in my faith and a person I can trust with a personal struggle I've been having. Could you spare some time for us to meet and discuss the possibility of an accountability relationship?"

Ideally, your partner will respond with both grace and loving conviction to help you break free from this stronghold. On the off chance that things don't work out, don't be discouraged. Rather, continue to pray and trust that God will connect you with the right person. Confessing your sins within an accountability relationship is a vitally important step in your journey. Since much of the power of your stronghold lies in its secrecy, your bold confession is the key to breaking its hold over you.

Exercise Regularly

While you might not consider them "spiritual" acts, similar to fasting, exercising and consuming a healthy diet are powerful seeds to sow if you want to reap a harvest of self-control. In his letter to the Corinthian church, Paul writes, " I discipline my body like an athlete, training it to do what it should. Otherwise, I fear that after preaching to others I myself might be disqualified" (1 Corinthians 9:27, NLT). This verse implies that Paul's physical training is yielding the spiritual benefit of endurance. Persevering through a difficult workout builds up your "discipline" muscles so that you can maintain self-control over physical impulses. Those post-workout endorphins are a nice bonus, too. Right?

Before sharing a few suggestions of my own, I'd like to share a quick disclaimer: Please consult with your doctor and/or nutritionist to create the best fitness plan for you. I am not offering professional fitness advice but sharing my experience about what has worked for me. With that in mind, I'd say start slowly with exercising if you've been living more of a sedentary lifestyle. Try some quick routines that will help you first improve your posture and flexibility. Later, when you can feel that your body has gradually become more flexible and limber, build your way up to more challenging workouts. My biggest tip with your diet is this: Drink more water! In my experience, drinking only water consistently throughout my day has drastically improved both my mental and physical health.

Spiritual Habit #2: Set Boundaries

There's a carpet that I'm not allowed to walk on in my mother's dining room—unless I'm barefoot. That rule is just one of the many boundaries she sets to protect her most prized possessions. There's a suede chair in her living room that only she can sit in. Simply Lemonade in the fridge I won't dare drink. China cups in cabinets I'm not bold enough to use, because if one breaks...Listen, you don't want to break one of Venus's glasses. And last, but certainly not least, there's a Shih Tzu in the backyard I can't chastise for being in the kitchen without mom rushing to his defense.

Though I love to tease my mom about her endless list of rules, she has successfully conditioned me to respect the things she loves. I know exactly where I may walk or sit in her house. I know which dishware to use and which to avoid. I don't always agree with the limitations she sets, but at the end of the day, I love my mom, so I respect her boundaries. I follow all her rules, and all her precious things *stay precious*, not dirtied, mistreated, or broken.

As we pursue purity, there are boundaries women battling lust must set to keep the most precious parts of us, *precious*. Setting boundaries protects us from self-destructive behavior and teaches others how to respect us in relationship. But where do we begin?

In the paragraphs that follow, I've outlined four practical areas where you can set boundaries to protect your sexual integrity. Notice that each vulnerability from the Spiritual Vulnerability Assessment falls within one of these key areas, so be prepared to refer back to the descriptions in the scoring section for more detailed and actionable advice in guarding each area.

Relationships

    Our connection with God is the basis of how we relate to others. When our emotional and spiritual needs are already met in Christ, we're less likely to impede on the healthy relational boundaries of others or allow trespassers to trample over our own. Since the quality of our intimacy with God is the heart and soul of our relationships with others, it's critically important that we safeguard our bond with our Creator above all else.

    We can practice prioritizing our relationship with God by clearly communicating which language and behaviors are considered out-of-bounds for ourselves and others. This will, of course, look differently depending on the individual and your relationship to him or her in a given season of your life. As a single, for example, you may ask a close friend to support your commitment to biblical purity by not pushing you to hook up with someone or participate in social gatherings where your convictions will be tested. You might communicate to a potential spouse that you're not going to be physically intimate with anyone until you're married. One wise boundary to implement during courtship and engagement is to minimize time alone in secluded places together. Finally, as a married woman, you may restrict conversations with flirty coworkers to public places and avoid contact as much as possible. These are just a few possible ways to protect yourself and others in relationship.

Entertainment

Set boundaries in your entertainment by committing to watching media and engaging in activities that promote biblical sexuality. *Wait. Hold up, Nia. You might as well say I can't watch, listen, or play anything.* I get it and if this is how you feel, I think you get it too. Hollywood movies and secular programming are saturated with sexual content. I want to ask you two questions to help put this sensitive subject in its proper perspective. What is *finding healthier alternatives* in light of a Savior who died for the sins we find entertaining? Can we even call having to watch movies without sex scenes *a sacrifice* in light of all that Christ has done for us?

Fortunately, we're living in something like the Christian renaissance of entertainment. Not only are there services such as *Pureflix*, filtering software such as *VidAngel*, and countless family-friendly YouTube channels, contemporary Christian artists such as V Rose, Tauren Wells, and shai linne (the lowercase MC) are consistently releasing albums that are highly competitive with renown secular artists. Why not consume content that will both entertain you and reinforce your biblical values?

Environment

One of my life-long ambitions is to be able to speak Japanese fluently. To achieve native-level proficiency, experts recommend that you immerse yourself in your target language daily. Ideally, I'd do this by settling my family into a cozy apartment in Osaka and spending countless coffee dates with my native Japanese friends, but until then…I'll have to cultivate an immersion experience for myself. So my bookcases are covered with Japanese textbooks and novels, my television is set to Japanese animations, my music playlist streams Japanese artists, and—at least once a week—I spend an hour speaking to a native Japanese tutor. In the same way, pursuing a biblically pure lifestyle requires us to immerse ourselves—so far as it depends on us—in an environment that facilitates this commitment.

Immerse yourself in a biblically pure lifestyle by setting boundaries in your environment. Since God has given you a spiritual makeover, why not give your home a transformation of its own? Take some time to create an environment that invites you to go into God's presence daily. Cleanse your space of anything that could cause you to stumble sexually, such as devices, pictures, or pornographic DVDs. Trash them. Avoid events and places, such as parties, clubs, stores, etc., where sexual sin is invited and encouraged, and instead, surround yourself with the good company of loved ones who will encourage you in reaching your goals.

Character

I probably shouldn't be confessing this here, but I still like to play "dress up." Fortunately, I don't have to purchase a new wardrobe every week or expend the effort of actually trying clothes on for myself, thanks to the paper doll dress up game on my phone. Essentially, you make progress as you compete with other fashionistas you meet throughout the game. First, you'll be introduced to a fashion trend via the storyline. To win your battles, you have to understand what style of clothes fits that trend. Then, you'll enter fashion-battles with your opponents to see whose outfit most conforms to that trend. This sequence of events is quite similar to how we come to set boundaries in our character.

Imagine your soul as the doll from my illustration. To win the battle for our devotion toward God, we have to pay close attention to and emulate the spiritual trend of God's perfectly good nature. The Bible says it like this: "Put on the new self, created after the likeness of God in true righteousness and holiness" (Ephesians 4:24, ESV). As you go about the mundane activities of your day, picture the decisions you make as clothing items. Before putting them on, ask yourself, *Does this selection conform to God's pattern of living?* Just imagine how this simple thought process would transform the literal clothes you wear, the words you speak, and how you conduct yourself among coworkers, neighbors, and friends. As ambassadors of Christ, these choices are an extension of our testimony about who He is. Because we love Him, let's seek to accurately communicate God's goodness in all that we do.

Spiritual Habit #3: Pursue Your Calling

My pastor often brags that his wife is a financial guru. During a sermon on personal finances, he told us about her reaction to a retail coupon she received in the mail. "Twenty percent off," she scoffed. "How about I save one hundred percent of my money by staying at home instead of buying clothes I don't need." I can't help but laugh when I think of my thrifty pastor's wife saying this, but she makes a good point. If you're saving your money, you're not wasting your money, right? Let's apply this same logic to our purity pursuit.

Just as *saving* money prevents us from *wasting* money, *pursuing our calling* prevents us from *being distracted by lust*. When I come into some surprise income, I confess I'm often tempted to blow it on luxuries I could go without, instead of saving it for a pinch situation. Similarly, as you cut out a lot of habits that lead to lust, you'll find yourself with extra time and energy. You certainly don't want to blow either on mindless tasks or endeavors that could potentially lead you back into a cycle of defeat. Instead, use your time, energy, and resources to invest in your God-given calling.

Paul teaches in Ephesians 2:10, that "we are God's masterpiece[s]. He has created us anew in Christ Jesus, so we can do the good things he planned for us long ago" (NLT). Along with the priceless gift of reconciliation with God, Christ conquered death on our behalf so that we could experience abundant life—life bursting at the seams with eternal significance right here, right now.

Since the majority of the practical application for this spiritual habit has already been covered in chapter five, I've offered three action items for your review. Invest in yourself and your God-given purpose by:

1. Using your gifts to serve your church family and your community.

2. Sharpening your skills and talents with for-

mal training (i.e. a class, online course, residency, internship, etc.).

3. Devoting time in your weekly schedule to working on goals related to your calling.

As we incorporate the three habits of sowing into the Spirit, setting boundaries, and pursuing our calling, we can rest assured that God will guarantee us a return on our investments. And just as wise investors are unlikely to pull out of a venture they've already poured significant cash into, the more we invest in our personal relationship with God, the harder it becomes for us to flippantly engage in sexual sin. Because the desires of our carnal nature and the desires of the Spirit are at odds, we cannot please them both (Galatians 5:17). Therefore, if you invest in the Spirit, you will defund sexual immorality, which produces weeds of sin that spring up and choke the life out of your relationship with God (Galatians 5:19-21).

YOU DID IT! BUT NOW WHAT?

If you've made it to these concluding paragraphs, it means you've just designed your own strategy for living out the purity lifestyle. Beloved, celebrate this moment because you now know where you're vulnerable to lust's attacks, how to defend yourself, and how to sow seeds of spiritual habits that will reap a harvest of holiness. But before I go, I want to remind you that what happens after you read these final sentences is what counts the most.

come home.

Strategy is important, but execution is essential to achieving the results you desire. After all, having a strategy is pointless if you fail to execute it. Yes, you know how to battle lust, but "knowing is half the battle," as G.I. Joe wisely said. Now's the time for you to take action. Schedule time to practice these spiritual habits you've learned. Share your strategy with a trusted friend or mentor who will hold you accountable to taking intentional, consistent action. Finally, pray through your strategy, asking God to supply you with the strength to follow through.

This strategy session is far from over. This is only the beginning of your new purity lifestyle. Ready? Set. Go!

7.
SUSTAIN THE PURITY LIFESTYLE

If you've played video games for any length of time, you're probably familiar with the phrase "rage quit." Rage quitting happens when—despite your best efforts—you can't overcome a hurdle in a game, so in a fit of *rage,* you *quit*. If we were chatting online, I'd insert a meme of a sore loser flipping a card game table or a disgruntled gamer taking a baseball bat to his gaming system. It's an amusing phenomenon that happens to the best of us salty gamers.

But let's say you've never picked up a game controller in your life. Maybe you can't identify with wanting to rage quit a video game, but perhaps—like me—you've wanted to rage quit sexual purity. Let me tell you about a time, not so long ago, when I would've blazed all of my efforts were it not for the grace of God.

It's a story of an experience that wounded me very deeply on both an emotional and spiritual level and impacted the way I related to leaders within my church family for a very long time. As I open up about some of the details of this event, I want you to understand both my motives for sharing and my desire not to victimize myself, nor villainize the people involved. As my story will demonstrate there's a strong possibility that along your journey of pursuing God that you will experience a flash flood of raging despair, depression, disappointment, and devastation. My hope is that in sharing my testimony you won't be caught off guard in your own experience or swept away in a violent current of unmet expectations and hurt. Instead, I pray that you'll secure yourself on higher ground—in the loving refuge of your Savior. Now, let me begin.

The worst of it began when I was called into the office of my pastor at that time, where I discovered my contract to become an official staff member was withdrawn because of a lack of church funds. While this was a *polite, non-confrontational* reason for being dismissed, it wasn't the truth of why he made the executive decision to dishonor our previous agreement. When the time came to announce these details to the church, leadership wasn't transparent with the congregation about why I was leaving. After two years of faithfully serving along my coworkers—with no one standing at my defense or calling out this injustice for what it was—I felt as if I was being neatly swept under a rug.

Though it wasn't how I hoped to leave, I was genuinely grateful to return home. It had long been my desire to go back in those last challenging months, and I imagined that the comfort of home was exactly what I needed…*until I actually got there.* I want to help you picture the frustration of my situation. Will you imagine with me having your own car, apartment, cell phone, and the average luxuries an everyday adult enjoys. Now, imagine that all of them have been stripped from you. Your bank account is in the negative. All your friends and spiritual mentors live in a college town four hours away. You don't have health insurance, and to top things off, you have to move back in with your parents. Think of that entire scenario as my welcome mat home. And yes, it's safe to assume that the entire transition left me feeling ultra-depressed.

That depression made me open to falling back into the self-destructive habits of my past. I started looking up past lovers on Facebook in hopes that we could reconnect. But by God's grace, I ran into many closed doors. As loneliness raged like a spiraling vortex within my soul, I grew desperate to fill the void—*with or without God.* After all, I reasoned, God was the One who had brought me into that desperate situation in the first place. I got hurt by the church while serving *Him.* I was completely broken and feeling washed up trying to do *His will.* At my breaking point, I sat on my bedroom's wooden floor, leaning against the wall, hugging my knees, and sobbing loud enough for my already panicked and anxious mother to hear. I remember announcing my anguish to God in prayer:

> *Wasn't Jesus supposed to make life easier?!*
> *Aren't You supposed to bless me when I make an effort to live for You?*
> *How did things get like this?*
> *How did I end up back at square one?*

Somehow, the honesty helped me come back to reality. *No,* I didn't want to abandon my pursuit of God or my commitment to sexual purity. I was just very hurt, very confused, and very desperate to be relieved of the pain I was submerged in. Right then, I prayed, *"*God, I'm so sorry, but if You don't do something right now, I'm going to blow it.*"* I wish I could say that God did some crazy, encouraging *thing*—like gave me a vision of my future, spoke some powerful word through the Spirit, or took away my heartbreak in that moment—but He didn't.

In fact, all I could resolve to do in that moment was hold on to that desire to keep going and wait until I could go to church that Sunday. I knew that if I could just fellowship with a group of believers, I would get the encouragement I needed to survive the pain. I longed for a community of Christ-followers who could understand and identify with the struggles I encountered in my faith-journey. So, I decided not to make any hasty decisions about quitting until I saw what God would do that Sunday. And I'm so glad I did because that decision changed my life.

I'm going to leave you with that cliffhanger for a moment before I tell you what God did that Sunday—before I tell you what God did when I decided that I loved *Him* too much to quit.

First, I'd like to shift the focus to you by asking, "Are *you* ready to rage quit sexual purity?" If you haven't already been there or aren't presently there now, the time when you do feel like quitting *will come.* The only question is this: Will you be ready for it?

Unfortunately, many of us fail to plan ahead for

our rage quit moments, but this is a major oversight in our efforts. Based on a poll I conducted online, hundreds of women battling lust reported that the number one time they feel like quitting sexual purity is after they relapse. Thus, it's critical to your success that you not only prepare for *moments you feel like quitting*, but *moments of failure as well.* Instead of waiting until we're ready to quit to figure out what to do, we must think through our responses to these scenarios ahead of time.

Over the next few pages, I'll walk you through how to prepare for temptation, what to do when you're ready to rage quit sexual purity and how to recover after you've fallen into sexual sin. By the end of our time together, you'll have a go-to game-plan for persevering through the hard moments ahead. Let's dig in.

PREPARING FOR TEMPTATION

Each week before the Philadelphia Eagles face a rival team, my favorite football player, Carson Wentz, watches the game film from previous games. He does this to get a handle on the other players, along with the coordinated plans his competitors execute to either score or defend against their foes. Once he's got a confident understanding of how the adversary operates, he uses his findings to prepare a plan in advance for defeating the team. This strategy of uncovering the enemy's tactics to get ready for the fight ahead easily applies to our fight against temptation as well.

Like these stand-offs between two NFL teams, as believers, we too are engaged in a conflict—a spiritual war against the believer's enemies, **the world** (the fallen systems that influence us to exclude God from our lives), **Satan**, and **our sinful desires** (Ephesians 2:2-3). Just as a football player watches game film to uncover the opposing team's tactics and prepare a strategy for victory, we too must be vigilant in recognizing the enemy's schemes against us and careful to think through how we'll overcome temptation.

Of course, this strategy goes both ways, as the enemy will definitely seek to hit us at our points of weakness as well (1 Peter 5:8). But this is all the more reason we must remain alert and prepared for when enticement attacks. Let's look at four biblical and down-to-earth tactics to employ before encountering temptation.

Stay Alert and Prayerful

One tactic of the enemy is to catch us off guard. For a soldier, her careful observation during her watch can mean the difference between life and death. In Mark 14:38, Jesus warns us that spiritual ambushes are inevitable and instructs us to remain watchful and engaged in prayer so that we will not give in to temptation. Though we may sincerely desire to honor God by exercising sexual integrity, like the soldier who eventually becomes weary and exhausted from carrying out her duties, we must recognize that our resistance will wane. This is why we need the supernatural empowerment of the Holy Spirit that comes through prayer to deny our sinful impulses. It's only through the Spirit's strengthening that we avoid the folly and danger of being caught sleeping by the enemy. Your simple request for sober-mindedness and strength may sound something like this:

> *Heavenly Father, please help me to recognize when temptation comes. Show me the escape route You promised to provide me in Your word (1 Corinthians 10:13). Please strengthen my resolve and keep me focused on the satisfaction and pleasure that comes from being in an intimate relationship with You. In Jesus' name, Amen.*

Don't Fight Without Your Armor

The enemy also wants to catch you unarmed and defenseless. This explains why the Bible encourages us to "put on all of God's armor so that [we] will be able to stand firm against all strategies of the devil" (Ephesians 6:11, NLT). Let's examine the components of God's armor:

- **First, we "stand our ground" by strapping on the "belt of truth and the body armor of God's righteousness" (Ephesians 6:14, NLT).** Just as without a belt, your pants are likely to fall and cause you to trip, without the wisdom of God to ground your life, you will easily fall for the enemy's deception. We put on this truth like body armor when we go beyond simply hearing God's word to applying it to our lives. Godly living protects us from the disciplinary consequences of foolish choices.

- **Next, we're instructed to slip into the**

"the peace that comes from the Good News" for our shoes so that we will be "fully prepared" for the fight (Ephesians 6:15, NLT). Like shoes, God has made us fit to stand in His presence and to run the race of faith through the gospel (Jude 1:24). Because Jesus lived a perfect, sinless life on our behalf, we're granted hope and joy and are delivered from the condemnation we rightly deserve. This good news is our banner victory, and we should be prepared to preach it to ourselves and the spiritually needy at all times.

- **With our shield of faith, we're fully equipped to stop the fiery arrows of the devil (Ephesians 6:16, NLT).** When we determine to believe that God's word is true and that He keeps His promises, the enemy's assaults, which are meant to kill those convictions, no longer scorch our confidence in God or char our hope to ash and dust.

- **Finally, to resist the enemy's deceptive tactics, we strap on the helmet of salvation "and take the sword of the Spirit, which is the word of God" (Ephesians 6:17, NLT).** The enemy loves to get into our heads by distorting the truth about WHO God is and WHO we are in Christ. Just as Jesus counters Satan's lies with a right understanding of these concepts from scripture, our thoughts must be informed by God's truth so that we are not defeated by the enemy's lies when we encounter them.

You may choose to activate this armor daily through the practice of prayer. Ask God to help you actively put on this armor so that these spiritual coverings will safeguard you in this battle for your affections.

Rehearse Saying "No"

Before my mother would enter a store with my sister and me, she would often pause in front of the entrance, look us square and the eyes, and say, "Now when we get into this store, don't ask me for anything." She wasn't trying to be mean or stingy. This was just her way of rehearsing the act of saying "no" to us before we entered inside and assailed her with a barrage of requests for candy, toys, and anything else that looked shiny and promising. Like my mom, you too need to get into the habit of rehearsing your "no."

In moments of boredom or quiet, consider any possible invitations to sin you may encounter and rehearse how you will say "no" should such a situation arise. How will you respond to the impulse to watch porn after a tiring day at work? How will you refuse the sexual advances of a coworker, friend, or fiancé? How will you reject the pressure from peers to deny God's design for our sexuality? Let's think through these scenarios before we confront them so that resistance will remain at the forefront of our minds and effort.

come home.

Flee, Flee, and Flee Some More

It's often said that "Where there's smoke there's fire." In other words, you don't have to stick around until the house collapses in flames to recognize the danger of sticking around. If you sense the threat of temptation, if it's trying to slip a foot over the threshold of your heart, then turn away from it. Slam the door and lock it behind you. Block the person's number from your phone. Don't watch that romantic comedy anymore. Drive in a separate car from your fiancé. Keep the office door open when you meet with a member of the opposite sex. Flee from sexual temptation; don't marinate in it (1 Corinthians 6:18).

Watching game film is pointless unless it informs the way you plan to play against the opposing team. In the same way, these tactics must inform the way we plan to respond to temptation if we hope to maintain our sexual integrity when sin attempts to seduce us into compromise.

WHAT TO DO WHEN YOU FEEL LIKE RAGE QUITTING SEXUAL PURITY

Behind every strong desire to quit sexual purity is an even stronger emotion. It could be lust, discouragement, loneliness, boredom—you name it! When those emotions consume us, we become like intoxicated drivers behind a car wheel, liable to destroy ourselves and anything caught in our paths. But how can we slow down and talk some sense into ourselves before we allow our emotions to set us back in our endeavors to pursue God?

Here are five practical steps to take when you feel like rage quitting sexual purity. (*Pssst!* A lot of this chapter's teaching builds upon what we've already covered in previous chapters, so I hope you've read through the material up to this point.)

Step 1: Acknowledge what you're feeling to God in prayer.

Recall the A.M.O.R. framework from chapter four. The "A" stands for "admit when you feel tempted and confess when you've fallen." When lust entices you to compromise your sexual integrity, make it known to God, and ask Him for the strength to resist temptation. Here's a template of a simple prayer to help you get started.

> *God, thank You for welcoming my honesty. Right now, I'm ready to fall back into [insert your sexual struggle]. Your word says that You will provide a means for me to flee temptation (1 Corinthians 10:13). God, please reveal my escape route and give me the strength to stand firm in You right now. Lord, I know that I can choose to fold, or I can maintain my integrity. I'm asking You to empower me through Your Spirit to do the right thing. In Jesus' name, Amen.*

come home.

Step 2: Remember your why.

In chapter five we discussed the relationship between your purity and your purpose in life. There we discovered that a "yes" to sexual temptation is a triumphant "no" to finding wholeness in Christ and fulfilling your purpose in life. Ask yourself how relapsing will affect your relationship with Christ. What is that calling you journaled about in chapter five? Consider how relapsing will affect your efforts and effectiveness in God's kingdom.

Step 3: Don't get comfortable with the thought of quitting.

As Christ-followers, we "quit" when we refuse to resist sin and habitually yield to temptation. If we're going to practice biblical purity, quitting is not an option. Because we know God is gracious, it's tempting to assume that we may give into sin and later repent. "By no means!" the apostle Paul cries. "How can we who died to sin still live in it?" (Romans 6:2, ESV) When we constantly abuse God's grace, we press the mute button on our conscience and become comfortable with walking in sin without conviction or repentance, which is uncharacteristic of a Christian (1 John 3:4-6).

Step 4: Remember the progress you've made.

You may be thinking, *What progress, Nia?* But I want to assure you that even if you're not X number of years free—heck, even if you're only two weeks free—of your sexual struggle, the fact that you're reading this book and making an effort to walk in repentance means you're making progress. Your progress may not be perfect—you may take two steps forward and one step back—but every effort counts. "Do not despise these small beginnings, for the Lord rejoices to see the work begin" (Zechariah 4:10a, ESV). Rest assured that God will bring to completion the good work He began in you, but you mustn't grow weary of doing good (Philippians 1:6, Galatians 6:9). Don't quit!

One creative way to document your journey is Bible journaling. Document your daily prayers, ah-ha moments from God's word, and encounters with temptation in a diary or notebook. Refer back to your entries to remember God's faithfulness along the way, reflect on times you successfully resisted sin, and learn from your failures.

Step 5: Do something else.

This last step is pretty straightforward. Instead of lingering in thought over how you could give into temptation, busy yourself with something else. Here's a short list of alternatives to get you started.

- Text or call your accountability partner.
- Bible journal.
- Clean up. (I don't care who you are. There's always something in your home that can be cleaned.)
- Hit up your local thrift store.
- Pick up a new hobby.

- Start an exercise routine.

Now that you've got a few suggestions to get you going, take this time to write out three alternatives you'd personally enjoy. Do these instead of giving in to sexual sin.

1. _____

2. _____

3. _____

One more thing! Feel free to refer back to those first three goals you set in chapter five to help you get started living out your calling. Consider working on those when you're being distracted by lust.

OOPS, I DID IT AGAIN

Alright, back to my story. So, when we left off, I decided that I would continue in purity until I could get to church that Sunday. So, what did God do when I got there? Well, first, as I expected, I received the encouragement and strength I needed to keep going, but something else happened too.

I was relieved to find out the church was within walking distance. Not having to ask my mom to drop me off anywhere at the time was personally a win for me. When I arrived, two young men were carrying out church signs to the grassy curb. The tallest and oldest of the two welcomed me and directed me inside. I couldn't help but notice he was incredibly attractive. However, I was determined not to be distracted from worship, so I headed for the sanctuary, convincing myself not to dwell on the kind gentleman along the way.

The fellow, as I discovered during the "walk around and randomly hug people while we play music in the background" time, was a twenty-five-year-old young man named Gerald. I could tell by how he carried himself that he was humble and intelligent, and I was so impressed when he mentioned he held a degree in mechanical engineering.

As my first month at the church played out, I discovered that there was more to Gerald than his caramel skin, Colgate smile, and athletic physique. He respected everyone around him. He faithfully served others, and he loved God. How'd I know? Instead of broadcasting my interest as I did with guys in the past, I decided to observe him silently from afar. (This was a promise I had made to God after going guy-crush crazy overseas.) During small group Bible studies, Gerald always contributed valuable and biblical points to the conversation. I was so impressed.

Long and very beautiful story cut short—after getting to know each other through phone conversations and *Maple Story* playthroughs for about the length of two weeks, we decided that we wanted to enter a courtship relationship that would eventually lead to marriage. Not your typical romance, I know. But we were both confident that it wasn't a coincidence that we shared so much in common, including the fact that we both desired to do long-term ministry in Japan.

But even though we considered our engagement a huge blessing, Gerald and I do not blissfully reminisce about this time. In fact, we rarely speak of that time because of the mutual regret those memories bring. What soured our engagement to the point where we barely mention it? Sexual sin. Between our engagement and the weeks leading up to our official wedding, Gerald and I compromised our sexual integrity. For the sake of not taking you there, I'll leave out the details about what we did and didn't do, but honestly, anything short of innocent, friendly gestures is unacceptable.

Even though it would've been easy to reason that since we would be married soon it wasn't a "big deal," Gerald was very adamant about repenting and abstaining from sexual immorality. I confess that I knew we were in the wrong, but until Gerald confronted me about this negative pattern of sin between us, I didn't take repentance seriously. His strong conviction made me realize just how deceived I had been about our compromises. After all God did for me, I didn't want to spiritually betray Him by cozying up with the very sin Christ died to free me from. So Gerald and I repented, took a step back, and set new boundaries to present each other as pure on our wedding day.

I'm sharing our failure with you because I want you to understand that 1) Purity matters in every season of your life, regardless of your relationship status; and 2) Just because I'm writing this book doesn't mean I'm immune to sexual temptation.

Like me, you may fail, but how you respond to failure will determine whether or not you learn and grow from it. It's tempting to think that once we've fallen back into lust, we might as well quit practicing purity because we've ruined our "good streak," but we have to let go of this all-or-nothing mentality. Just because you fail once, doesn't mean you have to stretch that failure into multiple failures. *You can recover.*

HOW TO RECOVER WHEN YOU FALL BACK INTO SEXUAL SIN

So what should you do if you relapse? How can you recover from your failure and continue pursuing purity? Below I've outlined four simple steps to help you restore intimacy with God, avoid the trap of yielding to sexual temptation after a setback, and learn from your failures so that you can persevere in purity long term.

Step 1: Repent.

John 1:9 reads, "If we confess our sins, he is faithful and just to forgive us our sins and to cleanse us from all unrighteousness" (ESV). Sin disrupts our relationship with God, so repentance is the perfect place to start when we've relapsed. The longer you try to suppress or deny your sin, the longer guilt and shame festers within you, keeping you effectively chained to your sin. Christ's work on the cross satisfied God's wrath on our behalf. Because He has justified us—legally declared us innocent—through His sacrifice, there is "now no condemnation for those who are in Christ Jesus" (Romans 8:1, ESV).

come home.

Step 2: Believe and accept that you are forgiven.

One of the biggest temptations after relapsing into sexual sin is to doubt that you are truly forgiven after you repent. Once again, I want to remind you of this powerful quote from Juli Slattery, clinical psychologist and president of Authentic Intimacy: "Forgiveness is a fact based on God's truth—not our feelings." Your own guilt and even the enemy will accuse you when you sin with the intent to hold your failures over you and paralyze you from experiencing God's grace (Revelation 12:10, Romans 8:33). But God is unchanging, and His word is true. When we place our faith in Christ and repent for our sin, we are completely forgiven and fully pleasing to God (Ephesians 1:7, Galatians 3:26). Our feelings of guilt can't disrupt that reality. So, don't doubt. Believe God and accept forgiveness and grace.

Step 3: Learn from your failure.

Instead of allowing your failure to discourage you, choose to learn and grow from it. Take some time to journal about the events and conditions leading up to that failure. Ask yourself what physical circumstances made your relapse possible? Identify any emotions or triggers that prompted you to engage in lust. After you've assessed how and why you failed, adjust your strategy, and institute new boundaries that will keep it from happening again. Consider sharing your findings with your accountability partner.

Step 4: Confess and be accountable.

Confession and accountability are critical aspects of overcoming the stronghold of sexual sin for a couple of reasons. Knowing another sister or brother in Christ is invested in our journey reminds us that we aren't alone. Accountability partners and church leadership can graciously walk us through consequences for our sin when we might otherwise continue without correction.

After giving in to sexual temptation, you should collaborate with your accountability partner. Bring your sin into the light, ask her for prayer, and discuss healthy, biblical ways to move forward from your relapse.

Repeat

As a video gamer, I've never loved having to repeat a failed mission or quest. I much prefer a good "speedrun," a quick and error-free play through a game from start to finish, over countless do-overs and retries. But you don't have to be a gamer to hate repetition.

After all, children don't want to repeat a grade in school. Athletes agonize when they must repeat championship runs. Heck, you may even groan when your DJ repeats the same song on the radio multiple times in one hour!

The point? In our culture, "repeats" aren't cool. They make us feel stagnant and left behind. Perhaps the most frustrating part about "repeats" is the feeling that you're starting over from square one.

As you pursue purity, you may come to a time when you may have to "repeat." (Recall the "R" of the

A.M.O.R. framework from chapter four.) It's possible that in a moment of weakness, you will give into sexual sin and afterward have to recommit to your initial efforts to fight lust. However, I want to challenge you if or when that time comes to think differently about "repeats."

Instead of viewing your "repeat" —your failure, repentance, and recommitment to biblical purity—as a setback, understand that as long as you recover, you're making forward progress in your walk with God. God doesn't frown at our "repeats." In fact, the scripture says, "The godly may trip seven times, but they will get up again" (Proverbs 24:16a, NLT). The Bible symbolically refers to the number seven as the number of completion. This fact emphasizes that the number of times the godly falls isn't important, but what pleases God is the godly person's persistence, her determination to get back up again after she slips.

If you haven't already slipped in your pursuit of purity, trust me: A time is coming when you'll be tempted to do so. Persevere in purity by thinking through your responses to these tough moments right now. But know that if you slip, all hope isn't lost. God's forgiveness and grace will be there to help you recover. From this moment forward, think of "repeat" as another way of saying you're ready to get back on your feet and back into the fight.

EPILOGUE
WELCOME HOME

Come inside. I've been waiting for the moment that you'd knock. Now, as I open the door and see you standing here on the cute welcome mat that I got from Hobby Lobby, I can barely hold in my excitement. I hope you're okay with hugs because I *have every intention of* giving you one.

Wait. Let's snap back into reality for a moment.

Sure, you may not physically be with me in the two-bedroom apartment I call home, but I so wish I could transport you here with me as we wrap up the final pages of this book together. So even if it's just in our imaginations, I hope that you'd accept this invitation into my home. We have three final questions to discuss as we continue to pursue sexual purity.

I've always considered the warm, scent of pumpkin spice candles to be one of the best greetings you could ever give a friend when they drop by for a visit. So, first, I'd let you know that I was sure to light one in every room, and after showing you where the bathroom is, I'd invite you into the living room.

Once my gray couch and glossy-leafed house plants came into view, we'd see the sunlight that lingers on my sage green curtains as day slowly gives way to night. We'd briefly take in the view from the windows, just as tall and long as me, and absorb the tranquility of the greenery outside. Then our bare feet would transition from the dark walnut textured floors to the woven fibers of my dining room carpet, where we'd settle down at the wooden farm table that doubles as our dinner table and my work desk.

Gerald would be in our bedroom playing a video game, and our one-and-a-half-year-old baby girl Gabby would be counting sheep. At last, it'd be you, me, and an untouched bag of Oreos. Personally, I can't think of better conditions for an impromptu coffee date. We'd feast on cookies and, in between each bite, share our biggest impressions from this week. I'd tell you how Gabby has become obsessed with watching it "rain, rain," and how my digital Ivy plant almost died of dehydration via my Plant Nanny app.

Finally, after a few laughs, we'd press into the deeper stuff—like how you're doing right now in your pursuit of biblical purity. Perhaps as you process and apply all that you've learned until now, you're wondering what it will look like finally to be free of this struggle. Perhaps you've wondered why—despite all your progress—your sexual integrity still feels so challenging to maintain. You might tell me how you question:

- Does being free from your sexual struggle mean that you will never feel tempted in this area again?

- If you fall back into this sin, does it mean that you're unrepentant?
- Are you able to deny your desires until you see real breakthrough?

First, I'd remind you how honored I am that you've continued with me to this point and that you've entrusted me with these questions. Considering the answers to them is critical because they will ultimately impact how we'll measure our success as we press onward to healthy, holy sexuality. Unrealistic expectations can kill our confidence and break our momentum, but having a down-to-earth sense of potential roadblocks will better prepare us to endure the hardships ahead. So, if just for a little while longer, I want to spend these last pages discussing these questions that may be weighing on your mind.

WILL I ALWAYS EXPERIENCE TEMPTATION IN THIS AREA OF MY LIFE?

Even though I love learning Japanese, the writing system has always been intimidating to me, specifically because I'd have to learn 2000 Chinese characters to read on a basic level. Recently, as I've stopped psyching myself out about the sheer quantity of characters I must learn and instead focused on exposing myself to them, I've seen a lot of progress. I can now read on a first-grade level, which is encouraging because now I know that I can keep improving.

In the same way, sexual temptation may still feel *difficult* to resist. But as you're exposed to it and consistently stand against it through the empowerment of God's Spirit and His word, you will inevitably become less defenseless against it. Certainly, we are all different and our struggles look different, but we have the same Holy Spirit—the same God—working and strengthening us to overcome enticement. Even if you wrestle temptation with a Goliath-intensity, as we—like David—actively trust God to deliver us by choosing to wage war on lust, He will help us slay this giant.

Even if you don't personally feel like you've made progress because you often still feel tempted in this area, remember that being tempted in-and-of-itself is not sin. Even Jesus was tempted—by Satan too, I might add—but He never acted on those temptations (Matthew 4). It's indulging in and yielding to our evil desires that produce sin (James 1:14).

Personally, I still encounter temptation on a weekly basis. However, after encountering and rejecting lust's enticement for so long, it's no longer the threat to my spiritual life it used to be. Of course, I must remain diligent in my efforts to guard my heart from sin's seduction because I'm not immune to temptation (1 Corinthians 10:12-13). Unfortunately, temptation itself is a reality we must continue to endure until we are united with Christ in heaven. There is no magic pill to make it go away, only the pursuit of holiness to keep it from mastering us.

IF I FALL BACK INTO THIS SIN, DOES IT MEAN I'M UNREPENTANT?

While it's definitely healthy to examine one's faith, especially when wrestling with habitual sin, I've found that many of us often confuse *being tempted* with *being unrepentant.* This is another trap Shame uses to keep us bound to our sin. Shame hinders us from progressing toward our freedom by causing us to doubt that Christ has ever delivered us from sin's grasp. When we lack the confidence that we are saved, we lack the faith we need to actively resist temptation. Only God's truth found in scripture can disarm Shame and teach us clearly how to wrestle well with sin and repent in those instances we fail.

When scripture speaks of an unrepentant sinner, it compares this person to a stiff-necked ox, unwilling to be led by its master. "The term was originally used to describe an ox that refused to be directed by the farmer's ox goad. When a farmer harnessed a team of oxen to a plow, he directed them by poking them lightly with a sharp spike on the heels or the neck to make them pick up speed or turn. An ox that refused to be directed in such a way by the farmer was referred to as 'stiff-necked.'" (What does the Bible, n.d.)

The inhabitants of Judah, whom the prophet Jeremiah urged to turn back to God countless times, fit this description of a "stiff-necked" people perfectly. Despite God's gracious warnings and constant calls to repentance, the people refused to listen and showed no remorse for their rebellious actions (Jeremiah 7:27, Jeremiah 44:1-6). From their example we discover that an unrepentant sinner:

- Refuses to turn away from sin and remains unresponsive to God's correction (1 John 1:6-7, 1 John 3:8-10).

- May ask for forgiveness with the intention to sin again (Titus 1:6, Romans 6:1-4).
- Feels no remorse or guilt concerning their sin (1 John 1:8).
- Is more concerned with escaping the consequences of their sin than pleasing God (2 Corinthians 7:10).

While *I cannot* peer into your heart to affirm your faith, *you can* humbly approach God and ask Him to reveal whether these descriptors are an accurate depiction of your posture toward Him. Humble submission coupled with an honest desire to draw close to God—not flee from sin's consequences —will illuminate the path that you must personally walk in your faith. That path may be one of recovery by confessing your sins when you fall and restoring intimacy with God by trusting His forgiveness. Or perhaps it's the path of surrender, where you choose to truly seeking God, not just better circumstances, by completely submitting to Him now.

However, know that whatever path you must take today, once you give your life to Christ, nothing can separate you from His great love (Romans 8:31-39). Reject the lies of shame and guilt and instead, embrace holy conviction that drives you back to our forgiving Savior. Determine today that you *will* persevere. Keep going. When you fall, rise again and cling to God's loving presence. He will never reject or abandon you along your journey but keep you and sustain you in every way as you submit to Him.

AM I ABLE TO DENY MY DESIRES UNTIL I SEE REAL BREAKTHROUGH?

I never fully appreciated the sacrifices my mother made for me until I had a child of my own. My labor pains testified of the great suffering *my mother* endured on *my behalf.* The late nights I spent patting my daughter's back and shushing her cries told me that she endured sleeplessness so that I could rest peacefully. My desire to place Gabrielle's needs before my own taught me that my mom endured scarcity so that I would lack nothing. But most incredibly, my own relationship with my baby girl has taught me that nothing my mother laid down for me felt like a sacrifice because of her immeasurable love for me.

Now as you consider every desire, every relationship, and every temptation you'll confront in the days ahead, ask yourself what will compel you to persevere? We cannot hope to resist indulging our sensual appetites if our reward isn't greater than what has been forfeited. Just as my mother was able to make difficult sacrifices compelled by her love for me, only our devotion to Christ can compel us to stand firm when lust and enticement invite us to yield to our sensual cravings.

At times the cost of loving Jesus may stretch you thin, but Christ isn't asking us to pay a price He has not already infinitely paid for us Himself. After experiencing the perfect love of His Father in heaven, Christ put on human flesh, bore humanity's sin, and became the object of God's wrath on our behalf. As Christ pleads in the Garden of Gethsemane for God to allow this cup of agony upon a cross to pass from Him (Matthew 26:36-46), it is not chiefly the anticipated physical pain that causes Him to pray with such anguish and blood. *It was the thought of being separated from His Father.* We know this because on the cross, Jesus does not cry out, "Father, why am I being tortured?" but "My God, my God, why have you abandoned me?" (Matthew 27:46, ESV). Upon the cross, Jesus denied Himself the most magnificent joy and the highest pleasure, the presence of His Father.

How did Jesus endure the ultimate display of self-denial on our behalf? In her book, *Gay Girl, Good God*, author Jackie Hill Perry answers:

> *Jesus didn't endure because He was strong; He was most likely at one of the weakest points of His humanity, but He endured because He loved His God. Therefore, He was fully committed to doing the will of God, no matter the cost. This love is what will help us persevere: a love that sees knowing God as the body's greatest pleasure.*
>
> *Even in tears, and pain, and difficulty, we keep fighting because we know being in His will is infinitely better than being in our own. And just like Jesus, we endure because we know joy will always be on the other side of obedience. So we look to Him, "The founder and perfecter of our faith, who for the joy that was set before him endured the cross, despising the shame, and is seated at the right hand of the throne of God" (Hebrews 12:2).* (2018, p. 125)

Jesus understands our weaknesses because He faced all of the same temptations we do, yet He did not sin (Hebrews 4:15, NLT). His love for His Father motivated Him to take up His cross and deny Himself. Now the ball is in our court. When we find ourselves mourning over the deceptive delights of disobedience, we have two choices: Will we treasure temporal, sensual pleasures that cannot satisfy us beyond the grave? Or will we reciprocate this incredible love that Christ has demonstrated for us through the empowerment of His Spirit?

Now back to our visit.

When the time came to wrap up our conversation, I would pull out my cell phone from pocket to share one of my favorite worship songs with you. After pressing the white, triangular icon to play "Available" by Elevation Worship, the calming melody would fill our ears. Together we'd sway as staccato piano notes bookend lyrics that speak to the *mindset* and *nature of loving affection toward Christ* that will sustain us until our race is finished:

> *"For the One who gave me life, nothing is a sacrifice."*

Will you be able to deny your desires until you see real breakthrough? Only if Christ's love becomes more attractive to you than the alluding pleasure of sexual sin. As the Holy Spirit renews our surrendered hearts and minds, God transforms our affections toward Him, enabling us to find our identity and complete satisfaction in His love above all else (Ezekiel 36:26). It

come home.

is this passionate love for Christ that "endures through every circumstance" (1 Corinthians 13:7).

THE JOURNEY CONTINUES

Beloved, as we'd leave my worn-down dining room table and I'd see you to the door, these words would be my final benediction.

This book was intentionally created to be a practical and biblical reference for you as you live the purity lifestyle. Please refer to the step-by-step guides, prayers, and teaching whenever you're struggling. In fact, I encourage you to go back and rework all its content from time to time to keep the principles and framework presented inside at the forefront of your mind.

Within the pages of this book, you've encountered a Call to Biblical Purity, the call to a life of pursuing God. You've been called to a life centered not on stricter self-disciplines or following a long list of rules about sex, but on pleasing God and cultivating intimacy with Him by choosing to walk in the Spirit. You have many reasons to refuse this call, and you are no doubt still working through them.

It's been my desire to be a mentor to you, to help equip, and guide you into a transforming and soul-satisfying lifestyle of purity, but only you can decide to take up this pursuit. Only you can decide if you will persevere through the trials that will come to test you and the enemy's attempts to discourage you. The four steps of the biblical purity framework are not one-time events. Instead, they are spiritual habits you will have to discipline yourself to practice regularly. In the days to come, you will definitely continue to:

- Embrace the purity mindset—so that your thoughts match Jesus' transformative work in your life.

- Find purpose in purity—so that you can live out your calling and achieve your maximum impact in God's kingdom.

- Live the purity lifestyle—so that your love for God influences the way you live.

- Sustain the purity lifestyle—so that you can persevere in purity.

I'm sure you still have many questions about living the purity lifestyle. Perhaps even questions that are more specific to your unique sexual struggle. We've only scratched the surface of our four-step purity framework. This is the reason I want to encourage you to go deeper with me by visiting TitaniaPaige.com where I have even more content for the Christian woman battling lust.

On the website you'll find virtual training, an invitation to the online Purpose in Purity Community, and the latest episodes of "The Purpose in Purity Podcast," where my guests and I have gracious conversations about how to overcome sexual strongholds and become the woman God created you to be.

Earlier I mentioned that my goal is to mentor you on your journey. As someone who recognizes the weight of responsibility a mentor carries, I want to stress that I am simply a sinner saved and sustained by God's grace. I wear no "S" on my chest. I have my own insecurities to battle and temptations to resist. I have to diligently practice the principles outlined in this book, just like you. I'm on this journey, too. Through writing this book, God has graciously given me an opportunity to encourage other women with my testimony and to share what I've learned.

My dream is to inspire women to find wholeness in Christ and to break free from lust's deadly grasp. My story demonstrates how God can take every single one of us—no matter where we've been or what we've done—and transform us, heal us, love us, and use us (including our past) to minister to others.

This book is a call-to-action. It's up to you and me to take up the pursuit of God by living out the purity lifestyle. As you leave my home—but not my heart—let's commit to this journey ahead together, with open hearts, humble spirits, and an insatiable thirst for God's love.

This book is my testimony.

Oh, beloved sister of mine, I can't wait to hear yours too.

SPIRITUAL VULNERABILITY ASSESSMENT

I wonder if, like me, you played Dodgeball in your elementary school. In the open space of the school gym, I felt so exposed. Without a barrier to shield me, my athletic classmates often targeted me and called "out" of the game. When it comes to battling lust, many of us are as vulnerable to lust's attacks as I was to the bright red ball we used to play Dodgeball.

I designed this Spiritual Vulnerability Assessment to help you discover areas in your life where you are susceptible to yielding to sexual temptation—areas where you lack shields to guard against lust's attacks. Strengthening these weak spots will help you dodge assaults on your sexual integrity and persevere when you feel attacked on all sides.

Before you begin, keep in mind that this isn't a test, so there are no wrong answers. What's most important is that you are completely honest in your selections so that you can receive the most valuable feedback. The statements below may signify a behavior, thought, or attitude. Begin by reading each of them. Then, using the key below, select the option that best describes your response. Try not to overthink your selections. As my grade school teacher used to say, "Your first choice is usually correct." Place the number representing your response in the blank beside each statement. If the statement doesn't apply to you (i.e., mention of a spouse), just write "7" to indicate "never."

1	2	3	4	5	6	7
Always	Very Often	Often	Sometimes	Seldom	Very Seldom	Never

1. ____ I ignore the Holy Spirit's conviction about lust.

2. ____ An accountability partner won't help me with my pursuit of purity.

3. ____ I communicate with my Ex often.

4. ____ My spouse doesn't care if I engage in lustful behaviors or if we indulge in lustful activities, such as porn, together.

5. ____ I am/was a victim of sexual abuse.

6. ____ Indulging in lust helps me relieve stress.

7. ____ The shame and guilt I feel after falling back into lust makes me feel powerless to stop.

Spiritual Vulnerability Assessment

8. ____ I turn to lust when I'm bored.

9. ____ I have often engaged in lustful behavior after drinking alcohol.

10. ____ I make myself available socially to attractive people.

11. ____ I often contemplate past lustful encounters.

12. ____ Many of my favorite songs contain content sexual verbiage and innuendos.

13. ____ As long as it's not hurting anyone else, I engage in lust.

14. ____ I love to blow off steam with my friends at local clubs.

15. ____ I indulge in lustful behaviors because I know God will forgive me later.

16. ____ My actions aren't so much "sin" as sexual expression.

17. ____ I am/was sexually active with a friend I connect with regularly.

18. ____ My spouse and I aren't intimate with each other on a regular basis.

19. ____ I am/was a victim of emotional abuse.

20. ____ When I experience insomnia, I often engage in lustful activities to help me sleep.

come home.

21. ____ I might as well binge in lustful behaviors if I have ruined a clean streak.

22. ____ Flirting with others and attracting sexual attention excites me.

23. ____ After using a recreational drug, I tend to seek out a sexual partner.

24. ____ Flirtatious conversations and small touches from attractive people excite me.

25. ____ I fantasize or entertain lustful scenarios in my mind.

26. ____ I often encounter sex scenes in the movies I watch.

27. ____ To me, indulging in lust is a personal form of self-care.

28. ____ It's okay to visit strip clubs now and then.

29. ____ I can't help it when I indulge in sexual sin.

30. ____ I'll only confess my sin if I get caught.

31. ____ I frequent dating and matchmaking websites.

32. ____ I am having/had an affair.

33. ____ I have/am engaged in non-consensual sex.

34. ____ When I'm feeling lonely or de-

pressed, engaging in lust comforts me.

35. ____ I think it's okay to indulge in lust briefly after a long period of abstinence.

36. ____ I envy most couples I know and see.

37. ____ I often place myself in compromising positions when I drink alcohol.

38. ____ I mostly surround myself with physically attractive people.

39. ____ It's okay to think lustful thoughts as long as you don't act on them.

40. ____ My favorite tv shows contain sexual content.

41. ____ I would be embarrassed to admit if/that I am a virgin.

42. ____ When I attend a party, it's not uncommon to see sexual dancing or people dressed immodestly.

43. ____ I can't change my sexual desires, so I should learn to embrace them.

44. ____ I am willing to confess my sins and accept the consequences of my actions.

45. ____ I can easily arrange sex (or cybersex) with someone.

46. ____ I am emotionally invested in a relationship with someone besides my spouse.

47. ____ I am/was a victim of physical abuse.

come home.

48. ____ Secretly engaging in lust, helps me maintain my virginity.

49. ____ I will always be addicted to lust, so there's no point in trying to stop.

50. ____ I'm often disappointed that I'm not in a relationship.

51. ____ When participating in a social drinking/smoking gathering, my friends encourage me to engage others sexually.

52. ____ When wearing a typical outfit, I can't bend low or reach high without revealing my stomach, breasts, or bottom.

53. ____ When I'm lonely, I reminisce about past lustful experiences.

54. ____ I enjoy reading erotic novels or graphic novels with sexual imagery.

55. ____ Having a lover would help me feel loved and worthwhile.

56. ____ It's hard to turn down an attractive person when my friends or others are watching me.

57. ____ I need to satisfy my physical and emotional needs with lustful activities.

58. ____ It's judgmental for others to tell me how to express my sexuality.

59. ____ It's difficult to walk away when a flirtatious person approaches me.

60. ____ Indulging privately in lust prevents me from cheating on my spouse.

61. ____ I was sexually betrayed or cheated on in the past.

62. ____ I enjoy the brief feeling of acceptance and intimacy I get from engaging in lust.

63. ____ Once I've fallen into sexual sin, I feel that I might as well continue.

64. ____ I often ignore opportunities to invest in myself so that I'm available to friends and peers.

65. ____ After using a recreational substance, I tend to have lustful thoughts.

66. ____ I often meet men (or attractive people) one-on-one for casual dates and hang outs.

67. ____ When I'm bored, I indulge in sexual fantasies.

68. ____ When I scroll through my social media feed, it isn't uncommon to find nudity or provocative photos and videos.

69. ____ If I expect to have a spouse/lover, I must be willing to bend some biblical commandments.

70. ____ I don't mind doing what it takes to be the center of attention.

come home.

SCORING YOUR ASSESSMENT

Follow these directions to calculate your score for each vulnerability, named at the top of each section below. In the empty blanks above the item numbers, write your corresponding numerical response (1-7). Finally, add each number and record the sum in the TOTAL box for each vulnerability.

LACK OF INTIMACY WITH GOD	WORLDLY SORROW	SEXUAL AVAILABILITY	POOR MARITAL HEALTH
ITEM 1	ITEM 2	ITEM 3	ITEM 4
ITEM 15	ITEM 16	ITEM 17	ITEM 18
ITEM 29	ITEM 30	ITEM 31	ITEM 32
ITEM 43	ITEM 44	ITEM 45	ITEM 46
ITEM 57	ITEM 58	ITEM 69	ITEM 60
TOTAL	TOTAL	TOTAL	TOTAL

SEXUAL TRAUMA	EMOTIONAL HAVEN	RELAPSE SURRENDER	LACK OF PURPOSE
ITEM 5	ITEM 6	ITEM 7	ITEM 8
ITEM 19	ITEM 20	ITEM 21	ITEM 22
ITEM 33	ITEM 34	ITEM 35	ITEM 36
ITEM 47	ITEM 48	ITEM 49	ITEM 50
ITEM 61	ITEM 62	ITEM 63	ITEM 64
TOTAL	TOTAL	TOTAL	TOTAL

Spiritual Vulnerability Assessment

RECREATIONAL SUBSTANCES	MODESTY	FANTASY & SOUL TIES
ITEM 9	ITEM 10	ITEM 11
ITEM 23	ITEM 24	ITEM 25
ITEM 37	ITEM 38	ITEM 39
ITEM 51	ITEM 52	ITEM 53
ITEM 65	ITEM 66	ITEM 67
TOTAL	TOTAL	TOTAL

ENTERTAINING SEXUALIZED CONTENT	CULTURAL SEXPECTATIONS	SOCIAL GATHERINGS
ITEM 12	ITEM 13	ITEM 14
ITEM 26	ITEM 27	ITEM 28
ITEM 40	ITEM 41	ITEM 42
ITEM 54	ITEM 55	ITEM 56
ITEM 68	ITEM 69	ITEM 70
TOTAL	TOTAL	TOTAL

Now compare each section against the key below to determine your "Guard Level" against each vulnerability. Please highlight the vulnerabilities that fall within the 0-13 range (or your three lowest scores). As you begin assessing and redesigning your lifestyle, your awareness of your most significant weaknesses will help know how to intentionally study God's word, pray for yourself, and make decisions that will strengthen your commitment to biblical purity.

come home.

Score Range	Guard Level
29-35	🛡🛡🛡🛡🛡 This area is secure. Keep up your guard, Sis!
24-28	🛡🛡🛡🛡 This area isn't often a temptation for you but stay alert.
19-23	🛡🛡🛡 This probably isn't where you're most vulnerable, but this area needs to be reinforced against lust's attacks.
14-18	🛡🛡 This area of your life is vulnerable to lust's attacks.
0-13	🛡 Lust often gains a foothold in your life through this vulnerability.

AREAS OF SPIRITUAL VULNERABILITY

Now that you've identified your biggest weaknesses, refer to the descriptions of each vulnerability below. I begin by defining each vulnerability and follow with practical examples and guidance for strengthening each area.

Lack of Intimacy with God

Cultivating an intimate relationship with God is essential to understanding His character and will for our lives. When we fail to spend time with God consistently, we are more susceptible to the enemy's deception and sin's enticement. A lack of intimacy with God primarily manifests in bad-self talk, a flawed biblical understanding, or an elevated view of worldly perspectives.

Self-talk such as "I'm unforgivable" or "I can't change" conflicts with scripture, which declares:

> "If anyone is in Christ, he is a new creation. The old has passed away; behold, the new has come" (2 Corinthians 5:17, ESV).

> "If we confess our sins, he is faithful and just to forgive us our sins and to cleanse us from all unrighteousness" (1 John 1:9, ESV).

When we doubt the Bible's authority, we resign to falling back into old sinful habits and abusing God's grace because we don't believe it applies to us. In Romans 15:16, we learn that change is possible because it is the Holy Spirit's ministry to us. Submitting our minds, emotions, and physical bodies to the authority of God's word helps us resist the lure of our sinful desires.

Strengthen your intimacy with God by pursuing

a deeper relationship with Him daily. Create a habit of reading God's word and journaling what you learn. Take any nagging thoughts or indecision to His word to find wisdom. Give thanks and lift your concerns to God through prayer. Sharpen your biblical understanding and experience Christ's love through the fellowship of fellow believers by joining and participating in gospel community.

Worldly Sorrow

It is one thing to regret sin and another thing to grieve it. What's the difference? Regret is consequence-centered, but grief is relationship-centered. Many regret sin after being caught in the act or receiving the consequences of their actions. But godly grief over your sin is demonstrated by a willingness to come clean and to take action to reconcile with the one you've offended.

Grieving over your sin isn't dressing in black and taking up a season of mourning every time you do something wrong. It's feeling the urgency to confess and repent of your sin so that you can restore fellowship with God. Without it, it's impossible to see lasting freedom from sexual immorality. Paul says it like this, "For godly grief produces a repentance that leads to salvation without regret, whereas worldly grief produces death." (2 Corinthians 7:10, ESV)

Have you ever heard someone blame others, past experiences, or unfavorable situations for sin? This victim's mentality is a common symptom of worldly sorrow. This failure to take ownership of personal sin conveniently perpetuates a cycle of sin—one where the sinner is never at fault and consequently never required to change.

If you've scored low in this area, take some time to discern if your grief is godly or worldly. Are you more frustrated about the consequences of your sin? Have you been hiding this sin from spiritual leaders because it may result in church discipline? Are you more depressed about being a "spiritual failure" in this area of your life—being imperfect—instead of offending God? Godly repentance doesn't prioritize pride or ego. This grief makes returning to intimacy with God its the top priority. It leads you to appeal to Christ for forgiveness and grace through confession, and humbly welcomes God's correction as well.

Sexual Availability

As its name implies, someone who is sexually available is easily accessible to potential sexual partners. Whether physically accessible due to proximity or virtually accessible via an electronic device, it's overextending yourself to the possibility of sex with others. A low score here indicates that you need to exercise discernment regarding your relationships, the places you frequent, and the social platforms you use to connect with others.

Exercising discernment will sometimes look like saying "no" to things that in-and-of-themselves are harmless. (1 Corinthians 10:23) When something begins to hinder our spiritual progress, we must let it go so that we remain free of lust's grasp. Has scrolling on Instagram spiraled into fantasizing about what you see? Bye, bye, Instagram. Has the show you've been watching been sprinkling in sex scenes? It's time to find another show. Has studying with the cute boy from class spiraled into making out with the cute boy from class? Find a friend to help you pass your exam.

Remove unnecessary temptation by eliminating relationships, activities, and groups where lust will not meet resistance. If you're thinking, "Does that mean I shouldn't hang out with so-and-so anymore?" Or, "Does that mean I should stop going to such-and-such place?" The fact that you questioned it highly indicates that this person or place isn't strengthening your desire to embrace purity. Block any possible routes —whether via people, places, or activities— that temptation can take to attack you. The less available you are to temptation, the less opportunity there'll be for you to fall.

Emotional Haven

Lust is your emotional haven when you turn to it instead of God when you feel stressed out, lonely, depressed, restless, unloved, or [you fill in the blank]. In this case, indulging in lust has become a "pill" that relieves your negative emotions. However, you can unlearn this conditioned behavior by creating a new habit of turning to God instead.

Remember when we learned about embracing the purity mindset with A.M.O.R. in chapter four? The "A" stands for admitting when we feel tempted and confessing when we've fallen. When you recognize a familiar negative emotion that often leads to sexual sin, immediately request strength and comfort from God through prayer.

> *God, I feel so [insert emotion] right now. It makes me want to [insert lustful behavior you usually turn to here]. Please comfort me, Holy Spirit, and give me the strength to resist this sin. Instead, satisfy me with Your loving presence. In Jesus' name, amen.*

Follow up this prayer with an activity that helps you return your focus to biblical purity. Perhaps you could meditate on an applicable scripture or sing some praise songs. Contemplate this routine ahead of time so that when moments like these come, you know exactly how to overcome your emotion-driven responses.

If you are physically with someone or in the presence of something presenting the temptation, flee. Grab your stuff and run out of the door, Sis. (Then, do everything else aforementioned.) It may not feel great at that moment, but later, you'll be so proud of yourself for not allowing your emotions to sabotage you.

Relapse Surrender

Relapse surrender is the habit of extending one failure into multiple lustful compromises. Sometimes it's that voice inside our heads that says "you'll never change" that leads us there. Other times, it's the temporary pleasure of sin that entices us to camp out in our failures. In the end, we shrug and say, "Well, I messed up, so I might as well go crazy."

Like those who treat lust like an emotional haven, women who struggle with relapse surrender must unlearn the ways they've conditioned themselves to react to failure. Instead of responding with more sexual sin after we relapse, we can create a new routine that reinitiates our purity pursuit. (Recall the "Repeat" step of the A.M.O.R. purity mindset in chapter four.) We can start by confessing our sin to God immediately through prayer, and later bring our actions into light with our accountability partner. It's also wise to ask yourself: "What do I usually say to myself to justify repeating that compromise?" Understanding your reasoning behind binging in lust will help you mark those thoughts as red flags, warning you that you are trying to "milk" your failure.

Remember that one mistake doesn't have to become a streak or a season of backsliding. Learning to recover from relapses is a part of the journey to lasting freedom.

Lack of Purpose

As we learned in chapter five, a lack of purity leads to a lack of purpose. Not only do we experience brokenness when lust distracts us, but we also miss out on the opportunities God gives us to exercise our spiritual gifts and talents. Here are a couple of ways a lack of purpose may manifest in your life:

- You spend a lot of time wishing you were in a relationship.

- You find it hard to be happy for others' success or romance.

- You make yourself available to socialize frequently, especially when there may be attractive people present.

- You lack an intentional plan to serve and point others back to God.
- You don't prioritize spending time with God.

Strengthen this area of your life by intentionally using your time and efforts to pursue your God-given purpose. In chapter five, we discussed how to uncover your calling, and you wrote down your first three goals in achieving your purpose. Incorporate time to achieve those goals within your weekly schedule. If you're bored enough to consider lust, it means you have free time you could be using to work out your calling.

Looking back on my own experience, I deeply regret how much time I spent on pity parties as a single. I hate that waited until I was married to go after a lot of my life-long goals. But you don't have to repeat my mistakes. Become debt-free. Travel to that country you've always wanted to visit. Break that record. Start that business or ministry. There is way more to who you are than your sexuality.

Recreational Substances

A low score here means that drinking or smoking might contribute to your lust problems. If alcohol "loosens you up," it'd be in your best interest not to drink at all. (Of course, the same applies to smoking, along with drugs of any kind.)

If you have a healthy, non-addictive relationship with alcohol, try limiting yourself to one modestly sized drink. But if you think you'll fold on this rule, forego drinking altogether. When the possibility of going drinking comes up in conversation, suggest an alternative activity, or B.Y.O.N. (bring your own non-alcoholic drink).

If you struggle with drug or alcohol addiction, please seek professional care and rehabilitation. As the loved one of an addict, I suggest faith-based rehabilitation centers such as Teen Challenge and Celebrate Recovery.

Modesty

If you've scored low in modesty, it's possible that you —whether intentionally or unintentionally— attract sexual attention with your behavior or appearance. Our devotion to Christ unveils our inner, hidden beauty as we reflect biblical modesty in our character and dress. (1 Timothy 2:9-10)

Our modesty is most often expressed in our relationships with others. When Paul instructs Timothy on how to treat others within the church, he writes: "Do not rebuke an older man but encourage him as you would a father, younger men as brothers, older women as mothers, younger women as sisters, in all purity." (1 Timothy 5:1-2, ESV) These verses imply that unless we enter marriage with someone, we should apply the relational boundaries of a blood relative to that individual. This conclusion has some alarming implications about flirtatious behavior and how we express affection within dating relationships.

You may be wondering, "How far am I allowed to go physically within a relationship?" While it's not uncommon for family members to kiss each other or to hold hands, I want to caution you against finding "the line." Because when you get caught up in trying to figure out where "the line" is, you miss the heart behind why God wants us to maintain physical purity in the first place.

Whether she desires to marry or not, it's the Christian woman's responsibility to present herself and her fellow saints (a spouse, her family, or her friends) as holy unto God. (1 Corinthians 6:19-20) She doesn't want to cause anyone to stumble by leading an individual into sin or willingly sinning with another. (Matthew 5:27-29) She glorifies God in her behavior by maintaining honest relationships with others.

Modesty in our appearance is equally important as our behavior. As women, we possess a natural desire to unveil our beauty, but we must remember that our appearance is an extension of our Christian witness. It's another way we can point others to Christ and draw attention to God, rather than ourselves. (1 Peter 3:3-4) In contrast, to dress immodestly is to wear what draws attention to you physically.

Let me be the first to confess that the habit of modest dress didn't come naturally to me. Around a year after receiving Christ —a season when I began regularly spending time with God— I realized that I could make more God-honoring fashion choices. The bend and reach test, along with the questions below, are simple guidelines that have helped me construct modest outfits ever since.

- Stand in front of a mirror.

- When you bend low, is your bottom exposed?
- When you reach high, does your waist show?
- Standing tall, does your neckline expose your cleavage?

Here are a few more fashion guidelines to consider. Be cautious of sleeveless tops that cleave right above your breast. Try to pull them closer to your collarbone. The more your chest and shoulders are exposed, the more accessible what's underneath appears. Also, if it's possible to see the outline of your underwear or private areas, consider clothing with a looser fit or fabric that leaves more to the imagination.

Fantasy & Soul Ties

Do you often entertain lustful thoughts of past sexual encounters? Perhaps you have a terrible habit of lustful fantasizing? Or maybe you're dealing with the pain of a severed soul-tie after ending a highly emotional and physical relationship with an ex. These are all effects of the spiritual vulnerabilities of fantasy and soul ties.

It's easy to downplay the severity of our sexual thoughts, but Christ invites us to love God with all of our heart, soul, strength, and mind. (Mark 12:30) We do this by meditating on "whatever is true, whatever is honorable, whatever is just, whatever is pure, whatever is lovely," and "whatever is commendable." "If there is any excellence, if there is anything worthy of praise, [we] think about these things." (Philippians 4:8, ESV)

Practical ways to overcome this vulnerability include prayer—asking God to cleanse your thought-life —as well as continually engaging your mind in activities that promote pure thoughts. A few of my favorite ways to encourage pure thoughts include listening to Christian hip-hop, studying the attributes of God, hand-lettering scripture, prayer journaling, and teaching the Bible. Get creative as you consider how to love God with your mind by honoring Him with your thoughts.

Entertaining Sexualized Content

We consume sexualized content when we expose our hearts to song lyrics, television, video games, novels, or any other form of entertainment that encourages lust. However, the more exposed we are to such content, the more we begin to view sin as natural and acceptable behavior. The danger of rewarding ourselves with sexualized content after a long day's work is that it reinforces the flesh's natural desire to please self, not God.

Open your Bible to Matthew 6:22, and you'll see that Jesus teaches us that the eye is the lamp of the body. "So, if your eye is healthy," He continues, "your whole body will be full of light. But if your eye is bad, your whole body will be full of darkness. If then the light in you is darkness, how great is the darkness!" (Matthew 6:22b-23, ESV)

We guard ourselves against media that caters to our sinful nature by establishing healthy guidelines for entertainment, purging what doesn't meet those standards, and finding healthy alternatives to enjoy instead. When considering your options, test them with Philippians 4:8. Ask yourself, "Is this content true?" Is it honorable, just, and pure? If not, find an alternative. Fortunately for us, there are countless quality sources of entertainment available on the internet.

Don't worry.

You are not going to be missing out on anything by filtering the content you consume, except for more opportunities to repeat old cycles of lust.

Cultural Sexpectations

We subscribe to cultural sexpectations when we allow secular views on sex to trump God's word in our lives. Popular culture should never inform our identity or sexuality as believers. As the Creator of both man and sex, only God can define what is sexually pure and what is not. Just as the stomach is meant for food, our bodies are "not meant for sexual immorality, but for the Lord, and the Lord for the body." (1 Corinthians 6:13b, ESV)

Want to get to the root of this problem? Ask yourself the following questions: Are you unfamiliar with the Bible and its practical implications for your identity and lifestyle? Do you trust that the Bible is "objective truth" —that it's entirely true for all people of all time? If you answered no to either of the former, you know where your trouble lies.

As you familiarize yourself with God's word and discover its reliability, you'll strengthen this point of weakness. I highly recommend Scott Duvall and Daniel Hay's *Journey into God's Word: Your Guide to Understanding and Applying the Bible*. It's a brief and unintimidating resource that will help you study the Bible with confidence.

Social Gatherings

While we are free in Christ to enjoy celebrations and the company of friends, we must do so within healthy boundaries that keep us from being swept up in the moment. I love the festive atmosphere of a party and chilling with my friends, but I know from experience that I must enjoy both with discretion. When I fail to exercise wisdom at social gatherings, the relaxed mood begins to translate into my decision-making.

Strengthen this area of your life by taking time to survey which social gatherings benefit you and which do not. "Can a man carry fire next to his chest and his clothes not be burned? Or can one walk on hot coals and his feet not be scorched?" (Proverbs 6:27-28, ESV) No way, right? So use discernment when deciding who you'll spend time with and how you'll relax with your friends. If your friends insist on doing something that could get you caught up, remember it's okay to say, "Not this time. I'll catch you another time."

Sexual Trauma

If you've experienced some form of sexual trauma, it may be contributing to the stronghold of sexual sin in your life. Dr. Slattery, the author of *Sex and the Single Girl*, told me in an interview that no one has ever healed in hiding. Pray and ask God to direct you to the right counselor to help you work through the healing process. If money is an issue, please consult with your local church. Many local churches offer free biblical counseling ministries or can refer you to local therapists that offer payment plans that meet your financial needs.

Poor Marital Health

When a marital relationship between two spouses becomes strained, sexual sin loves to rear its ugly head. If you're currently experiencing disconnection with your husband or you're perhaps engaging in sexual immorality together, I suggest reaching out as a couple to a biblical counselor or licensed therapist to help you both work through problems within your marriage. (This is perfectly normal. My husband and I also receive counseling from mentors at our church when necessary.)

Of course, this may be more difficult if your spouse isn't a Christian or refuses to participate in counseling. In this case, I suggest lifting your concerns to God in prayer and reaching out to a trusted mentor, biblical counselor, or therapist that could help you work out an approach suitable for your situation.

come home
STRATEGY GUIDE

Bonus Content for Your
Practical Application

INTRODUCTION TO THE STRATEGY GUIDE

The *Come Home Strategy Guide* is designed to show you practically how to establish the purity mindset and practice the spiritual habits of the purity lifestyle discussed throughout this book. But what is a strategy guide anyways?

Back in the nineties, strategy guides were instruction books that gave you the solutions to puzzles in video games. They essentially walked you through the tactics you'd need to master to score well and beat a game. I hope to do the same for you by showing you how to overcome lust with the resources inside this strategy guide.

Inside, I take away the guesswork in your transition into biblical purity by providing teaching, written declarations, and prayers tailored to your struggle. I also offer detailed guides on getting started with spiritual disciplines and include example routines for you to follow.

This bonus content is based on the biblical principles and promises available to believers revealed in God's word. If you're anything like me, you've read this book, and you're wondering, *What now? How do I begin thinking with a purity mindset or practicing these new and unfamiliar spiritual habits?* You'll find the answers to these questions and more as you implement the content within this strategy guide.

section one

RENOVATE YOUR THOUGHT-LIFE

Confronting the Lies that
Keep Us Bound
with God's Truth

RENOUNCE THE LIES AND DECLARE GOD'S TRUTH

In chapter four, Embracing the Purity Mindset, we established that only a mind governed by the Holy Spirit yields a heart transformed by Christ. While we are immediately accepted and forgiven by God when we become believers, renewing our minds to match this new life in Him will take time. As you grow in maturity, at times, you will experience thought-patterns that threaten to derail your efforts. Rejecting such thoughts and choosing instead to apply God's truth will be the keys to cultivating a renewed mind in Christ Jesus.

This first section of your strategy guide will address the four most reoccurring mental strongholds among Christian women battling lust. In a survey of a few hundred women, countless cited the overwhelming sense of God's rejection, guilt's condemnation, shame's paralysis, and temptation's enticement. To aid you in this battle for your mind, I've compiled a brief, biblical synopsis of each ensnaring thought, along with scripture-based declarations, and guided prayers. When your mind begins to spiral into either of these thought-patterns, you can prayerfully use these scriptural meditations to renounce the enemy's deception and declare your belief in God's truth.

During each prayer, I'll invite you to confess the truth of your current situation by openly confessing what sin you've done or desire to do out loud to God. In this way, we acknowledge we are wrong before God, not to shame ourselves, but to bring our sin into the light and be cleansed and forgiven by God. I'll also invite you to renounce thoughts, sins, or experiences that have had power over you spiritually, emotionally, or mentally. To "renounce" is to declare your abandonment of a belief or position. It is to say, "Jesus, I refuse to give this [thought, lie, experience] power over me any longer." Finally, I'll invite you to declare and believe the truth of God's word over yourself.

Please keep in mind that the power to experience freedom is not in the words themselves, but in your claiming the spiritual blessings available to you *in relationship with Christ*. (Ephesians 1:3) Jesus is the One who sets us free.

Finally, if you find these prayers and declarations to be helpful, I highly recommend that you go through Neil T. Anderson's *The Steps to Freedom in Christ*. His coaching within this short workbook inspires my presentation of the prayers and declarations that follow. In *The Steps to Freedom in Christ*, Neil offers twelve steps to help you resolve personal and spiritual conflicts. Its

LIE ONE: GOD'S REJECTION

Are you struggling to accept God's love for you because of sin or feelings of self-worthlessness? Maybe self-condemnation is crushing you like an unbearable load. Or perhaps you feel the enemy's accusations nipping at your soul. When fears of God's rejection and punishment overwhelm us, they reveal that we have not fully experienced God's perfect love. (1 John 4:18) However, God has given us a means of relieving these fears in the gospel of Jesus Christ.

"God showed how much he loved us by sending his one and only Son into the world so that we might have eternal life through him. This is real love—not that we loved God, but that he loved us and sent his Son as a sacrifice to take away our sins." (1 John 4:9-10) This is truth that applies specifically to you as God's child. Even in your sin, God loves you, and graciously provides the means for you to abide in His love through Christ. (Romans 5:8, John 15:9-10)

God's word reassures us that we are fully forgiven, accepted, and loved in Christ, but I believe you are here because —more than the head-knowledge of that love— you're desperately seeking an experience of His love right now. Let's go before God with this heartfelt petition using the declarations and prayer below.

Declarations of Truth

As you prepare to declare the biblical truths below, begin by writing on a separate piece of paper, the lies that come to mind at this moment. Verbally reject these lies by saying, "I renounce the lie that [*name the lie*] and announce the truth that [*insert biblical declaration*].

- God loved me before I ever reciprocated His affections toward me. (1 John 4:19)

- In my sin, God's love for me doesn't change. (Ephesians 2:4-5) His grace leads me to confess my sin, receive His forgiveness, and abide in His love by choosing to obey Him. (Romans 2:4)

- God has given me the Holy Spirit to fill my heart with his love. (Romans 5:5)

- I did not receive a spirit of slavery to fall back into the fear of God's condemnation. I have received the spirit of adoption as His daughter. (Romans 8:15)

- Nothing, not even my feelings of condemnation, can separate me from the love of Christ. (Romans 8:37-39)

- God's love for me endures forever and through every circumstance. (Psalm 136:26)

- God keeps no records of my wrongs but rejoices when I let truth do its work in my heart. He is seeking my welfare —even when He disciplines me. (1 Corinthians 13:6, Hebrews 12:6, Romans 8:28)

- God is never hidden from me. When I draw near to Him, He draws near to me. When I seek Him with all my heart, I will find Him. He will never abandon or forsake me. I am His beloved daughter forever. (Isaiah 41:10, Matthew 28:20, John 14:18)

Prayer

Lord, Your Word reassures me that there is nothing that can separate me from Your love, but I confess that at this moment, I'm struggling to believe this. Please remove any unbelief that I am made right with You because of Christ's sacrifice on my behalf. Make me confident in Your love by helping me to see myself through this new identity You have given me in Christ. God, I renounce the lie that I am unloved, unwanted, and unforgivable. I announce the truth that You fill my heart with Your love through the Holy Spirit. God, I pray that, as Your child, You will help me experience Your love right now. This is something I cannot work up on my own. It's only by the ministry of Your Spirit. Direct my heart into Your love and the secure and constant presence of Christ. Please help me to pursue this experience of Your love daily. Please give me

come home.

> *a greater measure of Your love here and now. In Jesus' name, amen.*

LIE TWO: GUILT'S CONDEMNATION

While guilt is how we typically feel after we sin, biblically speaking, "guilty" is the legal verdict we automatically assume as sinners apart from Christ. This emotional battle with guilt is defined by our feelings of deserved condemnation for our sin. But you, O Christian, can win this battle when you preach the entire gospel to yourself.

To rehearse only the reality of our sin and the wrath of God we rightfully deserve is to live with an incomplete perspective of how God relates to us in Christ. Beloved, you must see the whole picture of the gospel to have a healthy relationship with guilt.

You are justified by faith in Christ alone. (Romans 5:1) This means that though you may be guilty of sin, that guilt no longer leads to condemnation because Christ has already endured God's wrath for you on the cross. Instead of fearing God, in Christ, you can relate to God from a position of total blamelessness because Christ canceled out your debt and credited you with His perfectly obedient life. Since God has given you right standing with Himself, there is no one —not even yourself— that can bring a charge against you. (Romans 8:33)

Are you ready to reject the false guilt of condemnation to embrace the loving conviction of God's Spirit? Self-condemnation will always make you distance yourself from God, but godly grief will lead you to confess and repent so that you can experience the healing and forgiveness offered in Christ. Choose to see the complete and accurate picture of your guilt (expressed in the gospel) by using the declarations and prayer below.

Declarations of Truth

As you prepare to declare the biblical truths below, begin by writing on a separate piece of paper, the lies that come to mind at this moment. Verbally reject these lies by saying, "I renounce the lie that [*name the lie*] and announce the truth that [*insert biblical declaration*].

- Guilt does not have to reign over me because God is faithful to forgive me when I confess my sin to Him. (1 John 1:9)

- I don't have to fear God's wrath, because there is no condemnation for me in Jesus Christ. (Romans 8:1)

- God does not dwell on my past sin. He has no intention of holding it against me and doesn't change His perception of me, even when I yield to temptation. (Psalm 103:11-12)

- As a man, Jesus can sympathize with my struggle with sin, but as God, He was able to resist temptation so that His perfect life would apply to my own by faith. (Hebrews 4:15)

- I am a new creation in Christ Jesus. Therefore, any voice of guilt that declares I can't change is a lie. (2 Corinthians 5:17)

- Christ purifies my conscience from sin so that I can draw near to Him with the full assurance of His love in faith and so that I can serve Him. (Hebrews 9:14, Hebrews 10:22)
- God's grace is not dependent on my spiritual performance but freely secured by my faith in Christ. (Ephesians 2:8)
- I can have confidence in my salvation when I demonstrate godly grief by turning away from my sin and choosing obedience. (2 Corinthians 7:10-11)

Prayer

God, I whole-heartedly confess every sin I have committed and humbly ask that you would forgive me. I renounce the accusations of the enemy and my self-condemnation. I announce the truth that when I sincerely confess my sin to You, You are faithful to forgive me. Please teach me to treasure Your opinion of me above my own or others. Through Your Holy Spirit, show me how to honor your standards without viewing You as cold or unsympathetic to my struggles. Reveal Your loving and just character to me through Your

> *laws, including the law of grace through faith in Jesus Christ. Enable me to look to Jesus as the one who as bore my sin, rather than spiral into self-hatred when I fail. Break the endless cycle of self-fulfilling prophecy that results when I regularly rehearse the lies that I can't change. Empower me by faith to reject self-loathing so that I can see the real mercy, forgiveness, and restoration you extend toward me. Then, Father, give me a hopeful vision of who I am in Christ and the gifts you've given me to offer back to You in service. Through the guidance of the Holy Spirit, help me discern between the voices of condemnation (which compels me to remain isolated from You) and conviction (which compels me to come to You for forgiveness and restoration). In Jesus' name, amen.*

LIE THREE: SHAME'S PARALYSIS

Shame is the product of godly conviction twisted into debilitating guilt. When we sin, remorse and godly sorrow are the fruit of a healthy conscious. But when we refuse to confess our sin to God, that fruit begins to rot and decompose into shame. (Psalm 32:3) Regret over sin is a gift because it shows that your conscious is alive and compelling you to reconcile with God. But the enemy and our sin nature distort that conviction by casting doubt on God's love, the power of the cross, and the Holy Spirit's ability to change us. Those distortions may sound like thoughts such as:

- How does God expect me to give this up?
- Can God really forgive me after I have fallen into this sin so many times?
- I've tried to change, but it hasn't worked.

Shame also distorts our experiences of trauma, sexual betrayal, and abuse. When we keep our pain concealed, the enemy's lies, including the lies of our abuser(s), festers inside of us just as the guilt of unconfessed sin. However, this hidden pain not only changes how we relate to ourselves but warps our perception of God. Our doubts about God's character, coupled with fears of being rejected by Him, stand as a sturdy, emotional wall, separating us from Him. How can we come to God when it feels like shame has paralyzed us?

In Philippians 3:12-14, the apostle Paul gives us some insight into how he —who was once a passionate persecutor of the church— neutralized shame's command over him. In verse 13, Paul says that while Christ hasn't yet perfected him, he does "focus on this one thing: Forgetting the past and looking forward to what lies ahead." Disarming the memories of killing Christ-followers was only possible for Paul because He considered everything else —both his merits and his failures— worthless compared to what Christ did on the cross. (Philippians 3:1-10) He put no confidence in his actions, whether good or bad and completely trusted that in Christ he was reconciled to God. (Philippians 3:3)

Beloved, you must hold on to the progress you have already made. (Philippians 3:16) If you have trusted Christ to cleanse you and reconcile you to God, don't double back on your faith in Christ.

> *Wherever remembering our failures will help us fly to Christ, love Christ, rest in Christ, cherish grace, sing of mercy, serve with zeal, then let's get on with remembering and regretting. But wherever remembering begins to paralyze us with the weight of failure and remorse so that we don't love Christ more, or cherish grace more, or serve with greater energy, then let us forget and press on by the power of grace for the little time we have left. That's the main word: press on in faith toward the goal for the prize of the upward call of God in Christ. (Piper, 2020)*

Declarations of Truth

As you prepare to declare the biblical truths below, begin by writing on a separate piece of paper, the lies that come to mind at this moment. Verbally reject these lies by saying, "I renounce the lie that [*name the lie*] and announce the truth that [*insert biblical declaration*].

- I renounce my former way of life that was corrupted by lust and deception, and I invite the Holy Spirit to renew my thoughts and attitudes so that I can imitate the life of Jesus, my Savior. (Ephesians 4:22-24)

- Now that I belong to Christ, my old life is gone, and a new life has begun in Him! (2 Corinthians 5:17) I don't have to be enslaved by shame and regret because God has purchased my freedom with the blood of His Son and forgiven my sins. (Ephesians 1:7)

- Victory over my past is mine through Christ who loves me. My sins, disappointments, and traumatic experiences do not define me. (Romans 8:37)

- Christ alone defines my identity. I will not be persuaded by human thinking or the enemies' deception to think any differently. (Colossians 2:8)

- I am fully known, loved, accepted, and pleasing to God. (Luke 12:6-7, Romans 15:7) I am fearfully and wonderfully made and precious in His sight. His love for me will never run out. (Psalm 136:1)

- God handpicked me to bear the fruit of the Holy Spirit and reflect His holy nature. (Ephesians 1:4, John 15:16)

- Though I am a work in progress, God has gifted me, and I bring value to the body of Christ. (Romans 12:6-8) I won't second guest this because God is faithful, and He will bring the work He began in my heart to its completion. (Philippians 1:6)

- I refuse to let the lies of shame drive me away from my Father's loving presence any longer. I will come boldly to the throne of my gracious God. There I will receive His mercy, and I will find grace to help me when I need it most. (Hebrews 4:16)

Prayer

God, Your word says that it's for freedom that Christ set me free, so I must stand firm against the enemies' lies and my thoughts that condemn me when I sin. Lord, please forgive me for the ways I have intentionally and unintentionally valued my own opinion of myself above Yours. I renounce the lie that I am hopelessly unable to change and announce the truth that in Christ, I am a new creation. I renounce my feelings of inadequacy and self-hatred and declare the fact that I am deeply loved, fully pleasing, and totally excepted by You. God, please give me a new perspective of myself based on Your word so that my efforts to change are grounded in who You say I am, not the sum of my past failures. Show me how to be honest with You about how I struggle without fear that you will reject or condemn me.

come home.

Empower me to be patient and to show myself grace as I wait for my perception of myself to match Yours. Holy Spirit, please fill my heart until it overflows with the experience of God's love. His love and approval are all I need to press onward to what lies ahead. In Jesus' name, amen.

LIE FOUR: TEMPTATION'S ENTICEMENT

Chances are that you've opened up to this page because you are experiencing temptation. Let me begin by saying that experiencing temptation in-and-of-itself is not a sin.

When sin entered into the world, temptation became a natural part of the human experience. You should feel as much shame for experiencing temptation as you do for experiencing the law of gravity. And just as this physical law has no bearing on your identity, your temptations do not define who you are. Satan tempted Jesus himself, but this experience did not change Him—instead, it revealed the nature of His love and commitment to God. (Matthew 4) Our Savior did not give in to enticement. As Christ-followers, we must pattern our response to temptation after Jesus' example.

Before being tempted by Satan, Jesus regularly exercised the spiritual discipline of prayer. We, too, should pray that God would strengthen us to resist temptation in advance. Satan wants to catch you off guard to tempt you in your moment of weakness. (1 Peter 5:8) This is why, in the moments leading up to His crucifixion, Jesus told His disciples, "Pray that you will not give in to temptation" (James 4:7, NLT).

When Jesus is tempted by Satan, the deceiver and the father of lies, He triumphs over Satan with God's truth. But reciting scriptures isn't what enables Jesus to have victory. The power to overcome temptation comes in applying God's word. This is critical in our fight against temptation because applying God's word is what truly demonstrates whether we believe God's word is the highest authority in our lives. This is why we must do more than store a digital Bible on our phone. We must store God's word in our hearts! (Psalm 119:11)

As we conclude this brief study on Jesus' response to temptation, we find that Jesus' love and devotion to God are what ultimately motivates Him to maintain His integrity in the face of enticement. And the same must apply to us. Behavior modification, religious performance, and guilt trips will only get us so far. Only a love for Christ that sees knowing Him as our greatest pleasure will help us refuse our sinful cravings and find satisfaction in our Savior alone.

Declarations of Truth

As you prepare to declare the biblical truths below, begin by writing on a separate piece of paper, the lies that come to mind at this moment. Verbally reject these lies by saying, "I renounce the lie that [*name the lie*] and announce the truth that [*insert biblical declaration*].

- I understand that the enemy is waiting for an opportunity to entice me. Therefore, I will pray so that I do not yield to temptation. (Luke 4:13, Luke 22:40)
- When temptation comes, I will humble myself by recognizing that I am weak and susceptible to sin's seduction. I will resist Satan by fleeing lust's invitation and avoiding situations that could lead to compromise. (James 4:7)
- If Christ hasn't weeded out an experience of temptation, it means that I am capable of resisting it and that he will show me a way out so that I can endure it. (1 Corinthians 10:13)
- God does not tempt me, but he will allow the enemy to, so that my faith and endurance may mature. (James 1:2-4, James 1:13)
- Because Christ is my treasure, I will pursue righteous living, faithfulness, love, and peace, and flee the anything that stimulates lust within me. Whether it be books, video games, TV shows, people — I renounce anything that threatens my affections for God. (2 Timothy 2:2)
- The temporary bliss of temptation is not worth comparing to the everlasting pleasure of Christ's immeasurable love toward me. In His presence, I find my life and the

fullness of my joy. (Romans 8:18, Psalm 16:11)

- I can reject enticement because I know that joy is waiting on the other side of my obedience. Because God's love is better than life, I will praise Him and contemplate all that He's done for me as I lay down to sleep at night. (Psalm 63:3-6)

- When I fix my eyes on Christ, I can persevere on the journey ahead. Just as Jesus endured the cross for the joy of glorifying His Father. I will carry my cross, fully anticipating the complete satisfaction I will know in His love forever. (Hebrews 12:1-2)

Prayer

Father, I come before Your awesome throne, pleading that You would reveal my escape route from temptation in Jesus' name. Your word says that temptation comes when my desires entice me and drag me away. I renounce my desire for [insert the lustful desire] and announce the truth that only Christ can truly satisfy me. I reject the enemy's lies that I can find satisfaction and joy apart from You. I choose to devote my affections to Jesus alone, who loves me and denied Himself the pleasure of Your presence when He took the wrath

come home.

I deserved upon the cross. Please give me an insatiable hunger for Yourself through the ministry of the Holy Spirit. Then, as I delight myself in You, I trust that You will give me the desires of my heart. Finally, help me to see temptation's deception for what it is and don't allow me to return to my sin as a dog returns to its vomit. Lord, I humble myself now. I choose to resist Satan and his schemes for my life. Now in agreement with Your word, he must flee from my presence. In Jesus' name, amen.

section two

RENOVATE YOUR ROUTINES

Practicing the Essential
Spiritual Habits of the
Purity Lifestyle

ESTABLISH THE HABITS OF THE PURITY LIFESTYLE

Take a moment to consider how your typical day begins. Do you start with a shower? Or brush your teeth to dispel your morning breath? Whatever you do, this string of habits makes up your daily morning routine.

A routine is a series of habits that become second nature to you. You don't even have to think about getting them done. You simply switch over to autopilot and do them, because the rhythms of routine are ingrained in you.

In the pages that follow, I'll provide you with step-by-step guidelines for practicing the four spiritual habits of the purity lifestyle. My prayer is that with each new habit you establish, you will transition from a lifestyle that marginalizes God to one that prioritizes Him.

As Christ-followers, we want spending time with God, participating in gospel community, finding accountability, and disciplining our bodies to become second nature to us. But as much as we'd all love to change overnight, the reality is that these habits take time and a bit of practical effort to form.

As you get adjusted to these new rhythms of life, remember to show your self grace. "Do not despise these small beginnings, for the Lord rejoices to see the work begin" (Zechariah 4:10, NLT). Follow the Spirit's leading and trust that God will finish the good work He began in you. (Philippians 1:6)

HABIT ONE: SPENDING TIME WITH GOD

One of the best parts about falling in love is the experience of being pursued by your lover. From start to finish, this pursuit is vital for the endurance of any romance. This joy of expressing love and attraction toward one another is the heart of love. If we were to rip this heart —this mutual pursuit between two lovers— out of the chest of any relationship, love would grow cold and lifeless. Sadly, this is what happens within many believers' relationship with God.

Though our romance with God is spiritual and sacred, His pursuit of us and our mutual delight in Him is vital to preserving our affections for Him. While God never stops pursuing us, far too often, our passions for Him waver. I confess that, at times, I'm too distracted with my to-dos to slow down, worship God, and receive the fulfillment that comes from simply being in His presence. Can you relate?

When was the last time you pursued God? Are you

reciprocating His love? Chances are that if you are not seeking Him, your affections for Him may need some holy resuscitation. When we accept Jesus, God gives us a new heart fully capable of loving Him, but God won't force us to pursue Him. Cultivating intimacy with God is something He invites us to do ourselves: "Come close to God, and God will come close to you" (James 4:8, NLT). Just as an intimate relationship between two people isn't accidental, cultivating an intimate relationship with God will require intentionality and mutual effort on our end.

Spending time with God is how *we pursue Him* and *reciprocate His great love for us.* Romans 8:38-39 declares that there's nothing that can separate us from God's great love, don't you long to say the same for your affections toward Him? Then let's demonstrate this love with a commitment to spending time with Him daily. Let's get started.

HOW TO PRIORITIZE TIME WITH GOD

CHOOSE A TIME.

You're free to choose any time that works best for you, but I have found that it is best to meet with God in the morning before I get too busy, tired, or distracted. Do you work irregular shifts on your job? Are you a mom or caretaker with an impossible schedule? If mornings are bad or it's not possible to choose a consistent time, schedule your time around specific activities in your day. For new moms, that may be when your baby naps. For a first responder, it may be when you have your meals. Our God is personal. Do what's ideal for your situation.

Tips for Waking Up Early

- **Go to bed on time!** If you can just do this, then you'll be 70% of the way there. Seriously, this is so critical!
- **Set your alarm the hard way.** Set your alarm to the most annoying sound ever, and leave your phone walking distance from your bed. This way, you have to get up to turn off the horrible noise, and then you can roll into the next tip while you're up.
- **Wake up!** Are you still drowsy after waking? Instead of going straight into your devotional time, make up your bed, take a shower, brush your teeth, put on your clothes, etc. You could even grab a cup of tea or coffee to help you perk up.
- **Hydrate.** If you continue to feel drowsy, I suggest drinking a glass of water. Dehydration can make you sleepy, sis.

CHOOSE A PLACE.

When choosing a place to connect with God, make sure it's distraction-free. If you feel tempted to look at your phone, get on the computer, or watch TV, steer clear of rooms full of electronics. It's better to go in your bathroom during your devotional time than to go to your bedroom and become distracted. Avoid the bed, couch, a comfy chair, or any place you may end up falling asleep. You can dedicate a room, such as your closet, for your devotional time if you'd like.

HOW TO SPEND TIME WITH GOD

In the beginning, I thought my only obstacle to doing daily devotionals would be showing up. *You know, getting up on time and being conscious.* But after jumping that hurdle, I still had many questions. *When I spend time with God, what am I supposed to do? Should I try to pray the entire time or just read the Bible? How long should I do this?*

Confused and overwhelmed, I asked God to show me how to spend my devotional time with Him. After studying the scriptures and reading the testimonies of other Christians on devotions, I found this outline for quiet time to be fruitful and straightforward:

Scripture Reading → Meditation → Prayer

Perhaps you're unfamiliar with these three spiritual disciplines, but don't worry. In the next three sections, we'll cover them together.

SCRIPTURE READING

Have you ever overdrawn your bank account? Perhaps you made a large purchase without realizing you didn't have sufficient funds. So often, we do the same spiritually. We attempt to go forward in our days using strength we assume we have, but soon find ourselves weary and overwhelmed because our strength is spent. A negative bank account is troublesome, but how much more is an overdrawn soul? Before we go into our day, we need a spiritual deposit into our souls. But how do we do that?

In Matthew 4:4, Jesus declares, "People do not live by bread alone, but by every word that comes from the mouth of God" (NLT). God's word gives us life. Scripture reading is an excellent way to deposit life into your soul. But how should we approach God's word during our devotional time? Is it the same approach we use in Bible study?

During a devotional time, we practice a **devotional reading** of God's word, which differs from Bible study. To borrow an illustration from Pastor Tony Evans, compare Bible study to watching the national news and devotional reading to watching your local news. When we watch the national news, we hear the weather conditions and headlines that apply to the nation as a whole. However, the local news informs us of events and happenings closer to home.

During a Bible study, we practice an **exegetical reading** of God's word, studying verse-by-verse in the proper context to discern an overarching Biblical principle for all Christians. In contrast, the goal of devotional reading is our personal spiritual growth. We seek to experience God in the scriptures for ourselves, listening for conviction of sin, encouragement, and spiritual insight relevant to our lives.

Please take note that your devotional reading of God's word will never contradict any biblical principle discerned from an exegetical approach. An exegetical understanding of God's word should inform your devotional experience. At any rate, both reading experiences contribute to our spiritual growth, so we must do both regularly.

Devotional Scripture Reading

- **Begin with prayer:** The Bible is a spiritual book, and we must read it that way. The author of Hebrews says it like this: "For the word of God is living and active, sharper than any two-edged sword, piercing to the division of soul and of spirit, of joints and of marrow, and discerning the thoughts and intentions of the heart" (Hebrews 4:12).

    Since the Bible is God's word —written by human authors under the inspiration of the Holy Spirit— we want to enter our devotional time with a humble heart. Begin by asking God to remove any presuppositions you may bring to His word and give you understanding concerning the day's passage and its application in your life. Feel free to use the example prayer below if you're at a loss for words.

    "God, I thank You for giving me another day to serve You. Lord, as I open my Bible to read Your word today, please give me an understanding of it so that I

can apply it to my life. I look forward to hearing from You. Please give me a humble heart to hear what You are saying and help me respond in obedience. In Jesus' name, amen."

- **Read with anticipation:** Begin reading the Bible passage for that day. Take your time. Read the passage multiple times for understanding and with an attitude of expectancy. Anticipate God to speak to you through His word. Sometimes God encourages us. Sometimes He convicts us by making us aware of sin in our lives. Still other times, He gives us a message to help someone else. Since one of the primary ways we hear God speak is through His word, we mustn't rush through the passage.

- **Meditate on God's word:** Once God has impressed a verse or biblical principle from the passage on your heart, meditate on it. What has God shown you from the passage (or the devotional teaching for that day if applicable)? One way to meditate on what God has taught you from His word is to write about it in your journal. We'll cover meditation more in-depth in the following section.

- **Pray God's word:** When I'm in conversation with a close friend, I typically lean in to listen attentively to their every word. I may nod my head in agreement or move closer when my companion whispers. But once my friend has finished, she usually looks at me expectantly, awaiting my response.

Once God has spoken to us through His word, we have the opportunity to respond with obedience. One way to do this is by praying God's word. Ask God in prayer to help you apply what He has spoken to you. You may also want to praise God for the truths and promises found in the scripture that relate to your request.

Exegetical Scripture Reading

It's difficult to apply a message you don't understand. As I mentioned before, our exegetical reading of the Bible (or Bible study) informs our interpretation during our devotional reading. If you are unfamiliar with how to read the Bible exegetically, I've provided a short guide for you below. (These are the steps you would take for Bible study. Please use the devotional reading approach I explained above for your time with God.)

The Bible is a collection of 66 books with diverse genres ranging from poetry to law. With this in mind, we must know the author's message to the biblical audience before we attempt to apply it in our lives. The following is a 4-step process to discovering timeless biblical principles within a Bible passage (based on the "Interpretive Journey" found in J. Scott Duvall and J.

Daniel Hays' *Journey into God's Word* on pages 15-22, published by Zondervan Academic in Grand Rapids, Michigan in 2009).

- **Step One: Discover what the text meant to the original audience.** Read the passage and examine its context to uncover the author's message to the biblical audience. One of the simplest ways to do this is to read the verses before and after the passage. Consider the historical events taking place at the time or any cultural details relevant to that passage. Study Bibles, such as the *ESV Study Bible*, usually contain such information in the pages introducing each book of the Bible or in the commentary section located below the scripture.

- **Step Two: Consider the commonalities and differences between you and the original audience.** Understanding what distinguishes believers of all time from the biblical audience will help us avoid errors in applying the passages to our lives. Not every teaching or biblical account will apply to non-biblical audiences. The list below isn't exhaustive, but here are a few examples of things you may consider:

    » Covenant (Is the audience under the Old or New Testament?)
    » Culture (For example, you may ask, "Does this passage unfold during a fes-

tival?")
- » Situation (In this case, you may ask, "Is the audience preparing for war or witnessing a unique event?")

- **Step Three: Identify the timeless biblical principle within the passage.** Using what you know of the biblical audience, identify the teaching point that can be applied by all believers, regardless of time, culture, language, etc. Once you come up with this principle, make sure it doesn't contradict the whole teaching of the Bible. Your principle should align with biblical mandates.

- **Step Four: Determine the response to that principle.** Now that you've identified the timeless principle, it's time to respond by outlining ways you can apply that teaching to your life. Ask yourself how responding with obedience should impact your thought-life and actions.

MEDITATE ON GOD'S WORD

No, meditation doesn't involve chanting or "emptying" our minds. When we meditate, we take scripture and reflect on the truths presented in it. If you follow the devotional scripture reading method I mentioned before, you'll do some meditation on whatever passage you read. Here are a few more ways to consider meditating on scripture:

- **Put the verses on repeat.** Meditate on the scripture by repeating the verse(s) over and over, emphasizing different words each time. I do this for two reasons: to affirm its truth in my mind and to examine the verse from different angles, like a diamond under a jeweler's microscope.

- **Rewrite the scriptures.** One of my favorite ways to meditate on God's word is to rewrite the scriptures in my own words. I tend to daydream if I'm not careful, so writing the scripture in my own words helps me stay focused on what I'm learning from the passage.

- **Focus on application.** Think of ways you can apply the scripture's teaching in your own life.

- **Memorize scripture.** You can use flashcards or turn the verses into a tune. Whatever works for you!

- **Pray the scriptures.** Finally, you can meditate by praying the scripture in your own words.

PRAYER

The funny thing about prayer is it's so simple that it seems complicated at times. But don't freak out, *you can pray*. You just have to take some time to learn how. Even the disciples had to learn how to pray. In Matthew

6 and Luke 11, Jesus teaches them the Lord's Prayer. This prayer isn't a strict formula, but it does give us an idea of what to include in our prayers. Let's check out some suggested prayer components below:

- **Worship:** Recognize God's awesomeness in your own words and express thanks to Him. (Take your time and be specific when you express your gratitude.)

- **Confession:** Acknowledge your sins and ask God to forgive them. If you're convicted of some sin during your scripture reading, start there.

- **Requests:** Present your requests to God and ask Him to intercede on behalf of others.

- **Trust in God:** When you pray, recognize that God knows what's best for your life. No matter what happens, God is still in control.

- **Submission:** Recognize your spiritual neediness before God and that He has the final authority over your life. With that in mind, your prayers should reflect your desire to submit to Him in obedience.

If the thought of praying still intimidates you, you may feel tempted to spend a lot of time reading books about prayer before you get into it for yourself. Books about prayer are excellent resources, but I want to caution you about obsessing over how to pray "correctly."

If you are waiting to begin your prayer life after you think you've got it together, you may never start at all. Don't allow perfectionism to trick you into making it complicated. God is more concerned about you communing with Him through prayer. There's no reason why you can't continue to learn more about prayer as you go, so just pray. For the remainder of this section on prayer, I'll provide some helpful guidelines to help you get started.

Helpful Prayer Guidelines

- **Prayer is a conversation with God.** I would scissor-kick my husband if he went on a trip and didn't call me while he was gone. I love him a lot, so I want to keep in touch with him. God wants the same from us. He may not be far from us, but we can sure get far from Him spiritually when we don't speak to Him or fail to acknowledge His presence. When we pray, Jesus tells us to say, "Our Father." We're not just talking to some far-away entity, but the living God who is active and present in our everyday lives.

- **Pray in Private.** Of course, there are times that we'll pray in public with other Christians, but when you're praying alone, do it in secret. For example, if you go on a prayer walk around your neighborhood, you don't have to shout your prayer along the sidewalk so that everyone can hear you. Pray silently or go behind closed doors. This time is about you communing with God, not trying to impress other people.

- **When you pray, be yourself.** Don't try to change the way you speak when you pray. For example, you don't have to pray using "thee" or "thou." Just talk the way you usually would in conversation. That means you don't have to fill in every moment of your prayer with a "Yes, Lord" or "Father God." It's okay to have some moments of silence in the mix.

- **It's not mandatory to keep a particular posture when you pray.** Some people like to lay prostrate when they pray. You do this when you lie face down on the floor with your arms spread out at your sides. King David often did this when He prayed. Your posture can be a way of humbling yourself before God, but no verse requires us to lay, sit, stand, or whatever when we pray. It's really a matter of personal preference and conviction. I would like to be able to lay prostrate when I pray in the mornings, but the truth is I fall asleep when I do that. The most important thing is that you have quality time with God. So, run and pray, stand and pray, sit Indian-style, and pray, whatever keeps you conscious and focused on God.

- **God hears short and simple prayers.** Do

you feel like you have to pray for hours, or else your prayers are not up to par? That's not the case. Jesus himself says that God will not hear us any better than He already does just because we pray longer. (Matthew 6:7) Even the prayer that Christ taught the disciples was short and sweet. Simply pray as long as you feel led to do so.

- **Don't shrink God in your prayers.** When you pray, remember that nothing is impossible for God. So, don't pray as if your problems are bigger than God. Pray as if your problems are pebbles beneath His feet.

- **Be persistent in prayer.** Just because God hasn't answered your prayer as quickly as you wanted Him to or exactly how you wanted Him to, doesn't mean that you should stop praying. Keep asking and keep knocking, God will reply. It won't always be the answer you want, but God works everything out for the good of those who love Him and are called according to His purpose. (Romans 8:28)

HABIT 2:
PARTICIPATE IN GOSPEL COMMUNITY

In Matthew 16:18, Jesus declares that the church belongs to Him. Metaphorically speaking, Jesus is the head, and we are His body's other physical members. Christ expects us to embrace our identity as His arms, legs, hands, and feet because gospel community is ultimately His design. (1 Timothy 3:15)

God formed the church to help us grow and stay encouraged in our faith. Teachers often say that "It takes a village to raise a child," and the same applies *spiritually* as well. Each member of Christ's body brings something to the table, and the entire body benefits from each other's spiritual gifts as a whole. (1 Corinthians 12) Through church leadership's Biblical teaching, we learn to apply God's word and grow spiritually. Fellowship with other believers strengthens and comforts us. (Ephesians 4:12) When we live together like a city shining on a hill, unbelievers will see our light, and, most importantly, they will see Christ in us. (Matthew 5:13-16, John 8:12)

If you're new to this concept of belonging to a local church, I've provided some steps for choosing a church below. (For more information about church membership, I highly suggest Thom S. Rainer's, *I Am a Church Member: Discovering the Attitude that Makes the Difference.*)

HOW TO CHOOSE A CHURCH?

1. **Start by locating local churches.** Ask the mature Christians in your life where they attend church or google "churches near me." I also recommend the 9Marks Church Search tool, access it at www.9marks.org/church-search/. After you've found some potential churches, ask God to show you which church would be a good fit for you. You are free to go to a church that's far if you're willing to make the commute, but that would make it difficult for you to serve their community with them. You also have to consider if you could make it there on time for services, especially if you have a habit of oversleeping or there's traffic.

2. **Understand each church's beliefs about Jesus and the gospel.** If the church has a website, search the site for something called a "statement of belief." Sometimes they jazz it up and call it something like "What We

come home.

Believe" or "Our Beliefs." The statement of belief is where you can check out what they actually teach and preach there. Please read it all the way through. You don't want to join the church and later discover that they believe something unbiblical.

3. You can also get a feel for the congregation's beliefs by listening to the pastor's sermons. Many churches host their sermons on their website or post them on their Facebook page. If the church doesn't have a website, ask a leader for a copy of their statement of faith when you visit in person. Or ask the leader directly about their doctrine or Bible teachings for yourself. Any leader there should be able to answer questions like: "Do you believe Jesus was the Son of God?"; "Could you share the gospel (as this church believes and teaches it) with me?"; and so on. Statements like "Jesus was not the Son of God" are a HUGE red flag. Learn more about the nine marks of a healthy church by visiting www.9marks. org/about/the-nine-marks/.

4. **Visit your top picks.** Go and experience worship at the churches that appeal to you (and your family). You won't understand everything about a church from one visit, so it helps to visit two or three times to get a clear picture of what they do consistently. I also recommend joining a small group

or Bible study with the members. Here are some helpful questions to consider when choosing a church:

- » Do the members greet you warmly?
- » Is the service conducted with respect and reverence for God?
- » Is there a children's ministry or any accommodations for nursing mothers or babies? (Optional)
- » What's the structure of the church? Is there a senior pastor along with a team of elders?
- » Do the members live in a manner that honors God?
- » Are there opportunities to meet with members outside of corporate worship?
- » Can you see yourself serving in some area at this church? Are there people who could potentially mentor you or teach you how to grow in the faith?
- » Is this church involved in missions or evangelism? Do they serve in their community?

5. **Prayerfully narrow your choices down to one church, and contact church leadership to take the next step towards membership.** Ask God which church He would have you join. Consider the experiences you have had with God's word and where you think the Holy Spirit is lead-

ing you. Once you've made your decision, contact church leadership, and ask them about the next steps to become a member.

Great churches will excel in the visitor to member transition in a few ways. They will have an interview process to confirm that you believe and understand the gospel. They may ask you how you became a Christian or some questions to confirm that you understand the gospel. The leadership may also ask you to receive baptism if you haven't already done so.

Great churches will also give you an orientation to introduce the church's history, staff, doctrinal beliefs, and membership expectations. Finally, great churches treat each other like family and hold each other accountable. If you are a new believer, they may pair you up with another believer to help you grow in your understanding of what it means to live for Christ. If your church does all of that, holds to biblical truths, loves well, and serves the community, you've found yourself a gem.

6. **Become a member of the church.** After you've completed the membership process, the church leadership will present you as a new member of the church. (Based on Acts 8:18-24, this process should never require any monetary payment.) Make every effort

to fulfill your role as a member, as outlined in scripture. Together, you and your church family should strive to firmly, yet lovingly, hold each other accountable to Christ's teachings.

HABIT 3:
ENTER AN ACCOUNTABILITY RELATIONSHIP

Perhaps, like me, when you hear the word accountability, you envision New Year's Resolutions of losing weight. Only by the third week of January, neither you nor your partner is exercising. And *dieting?* Why put yourself through the torture, right?

Despite the countless failed resolutions and broken vows, accountability partnerships *do* work —under the right conditions. As someone who's experienced the good, the bad, and the ugly of accountability partnerships, my goal for today is to share with you what works.

You may be reading this and dread the thought of bringing your struggle to light with another believer. But secrecy and hidden sin are the perfect breeding grounds for guilt and shame. Confessing our sin and asking for the prayers and accountability of mature Christians is a powerful way to begin tearing down the stronghold of sexual immorality in our lives. But there is more to accountability than strength in numbers. Let's discover why Christian accountably is so essential to our fight against lust.

WHY ACCOUNTABILITY?

Accountability is a biblical concept the scriptures encourage us to practice. (James 5:16) The Bible calls us to confess our sins to one another, pray for each other, gently correct each other, and to comfort one another when we repent. (Galatians 6:1-5)

Not only is accountability endorsed by the Bible, but it offers practical benefits as well. Statistically, having an accountability partner is said to increase the odds of achieving your goal to 95%. For some, accountability motivates them to succeed because they don't wish to disappoint their partner. Finally, many find the new insight and encouragement their partners offer give them the push they need to persevere.

Unhelpful Substitutes

Healthy and transforming accountability partnerships require transparency, and honestly, this feels unnatural, especially when you've been hiding behind the façade of "a Christian good-girl." As an alternative, I've witnessed many Christian women turning to anonymous confessions online—others email ministry leaders like me, with their stories. These pathways are rarely helpful because there's no real way for the confessor to be held accountable.

Accountability is a two-way street. You must be willing to be transparent, and your partner must be able to coach you in meeting God's standard. Avoid these useless substitutes by preparing to offer the level of openness you'll need before seeking a partner to hold you accountable.

CHOOSING AN ACCOUNTABILITY PARTNER

So what should you look for in an accountability partner? Begin by making a list of people available in your network or sphere of influence. Then work your way through the suggested criteria below. (Please be sure to engage the Lord in prayer as you do so, asking Him to reveal who'd be the best fit for you.)

Choose a Mature Christian

It's essential that your partner shares your core beliefs concerning God's design for sexuality and that she can provide you with biblical counsel. Preferably, a Christian that has not or no longer shares your sexual struggle would be best. Also, consider whether she consistently reads God's word and is seeking to honor Christ daily —not just at church.

Choose Someone You Trust

Make sure the person you confide in is trustworthy and able to keep your discussion confidential. Ask yourself, "Can I speak openly with this person about my situation?"

Choose Someone of the Same Gender

It's unwise to discuss sexual matters with someone of the opposite sex. (Let's not forget that our accountability partners are also humans that wrestle with a sin nature of their own.) If you struggle with same-sex attraction, exercise discernment by approaching a female friend who won't distract you from your goal.

Choose a Coach, Not an Officer

Not literally, of course. It would be best if you had an accountability partner that gently corrects when necessary but isn't waiting for you to slip up so they can condemn you. The right partner will encourage you to take responsibility for your sin while helping you to cling to God's forgiveness and grace.

Finally, if you are considering making your husband your accountability partner, understand that it may be hard for him to give you objective advice. Of course, you should involve your spouse as much as you both agree is healthy, but I would have at least one person outside of my marriage to hold me accountable.

RECOMMENDATIONS FOR A SUCCESSFUL PARTNERSHIP

Once you've approached your potential partner and she agrees to support you, you'll want to do a few things to ensure your success. Here are my recommendations to ensure things flow as smoothly as possible.

Set Your Expectations

Take an afternoon to grab coffee with your accountability partner to set the expectations for your partnership. Clearly define how you would like your partner to hold you accountable. Ask her what she would need from you to best support you. Together, decide whether you'll chat once a week, do a Bible study together, or use an accountability software. Now's the time to ask when you can contact them if you're feeling tempted or need prayer or encouragement.

Be Transparent

Alright, you're probably tired of hearing this, but this is a dead horse that I must beat. Without transparency, there's no way for your accountability partner to help you. So please, be ready to share if you're struggling. That's why she is there —to support you and help you gain victory over this sin.

Communicate

If some aspect of your accountability relationship needs to change, communicate that with your partner, especially time-specific or logistical changes. If you know ahead of time you won't be able to meet on your regular day, call your partner ahead to reschedule your meeting. Respect each other's' time and efforts by responding to communication promptly, even if it's to say, "Hey, I got your message. I'll be in touch soon."

Alright, sis. I hope you found these guidelines and tips helpful as you seek an accountability partner. If you'd like to dive deeper into today's discussion, I highly recommend Covenant Eyes' *Coming Clean: Overcoming Lust Through Biblical Accountability* pdf download, available at www.CovenantEyes.com/Accountability-Partner-ebook/. Perhaps you could even read through this e-book with your partner.

HABIT 4.
EXERCISE REGULARLY

> *Do not waste time arguing over godless ideas and old wives' tales. Instead, train yourself to be godly. "Physical training is good, but training for godliness is much better, promising benefits in this life and in the life to come." (Philippians 4:7-8, NLT)*

Perhaps after reading the title of this final spiritual habit, exercise regularly, you're wondering, *what does exercise have to do with pursuing biblical purity?* Moreover, doesn't Philippians 4:7-8 tell us that *"training for godliness"* is better than *"physical training?"* In a brief Bible study on these verses, GotQuestions.org concludes:

> *While the focus of these Scriptures is not physical exercise, the fact that Paul uses athletic terminology to teach us spiritual truths indicates that Paul viewed*

> *physical exercise, and even competition, in a positive light. We are both physical and spiritual beings. While the spiritual aspect of our being is, biblically speaking, more important, we are to neglect neither the spiritual or physical aspects of our health." (Should a Christian, n.d.)*

Our bodies are the temple of the Holy Spirit, who dwells inside of us. Therefore, we must steward them well, both physically and spiritually. To this point, Paul instructs the Corinthian church to "run from sexual sin" (1 Corinthians 6:18, NLT).

> *No other sin so clearly affects the body as this one does. For sexual immorality is a sin against your own body. Don't you realize that your body is the temple of the Holy Spirit, who lives in you and was given to you by God? You do not belong to yourself, for God bought you with a high price. So you must honor God with your body. (1 Corinthians 6:18-20, NLT)*

As Paul mentioned before, sexual immorality not only affects us spiritually but physically as well.

If you've done any length of online research on overcoming pornography addiction, chances are that you've discovered pornography's addictive influence on the body. Fight the New Drug, a secular nonprofit organization dedicated to raising awareness of pornography's harmful effects reports:

> *Studies have shown that porn stimu-*

lates the same areas of the brain as addictive drugs, making the brain release the same chemicals. And just like drugs, porn triggers pathways in the brain that cause craving, leading users back for more and more extreme "hits" to get high. (How porn affects, 2017)

With this in mind, let's also consider the benefits of exercise in our recovery from addictive sexual sins. Regular exercise:

- Helps reduce your sexual impulses.
- Relieves stress that would otherwise lead to setbacks.
- Releases mood regulators such as endorphins, dopamine, and serotonin.
- Improves your mental health and physical endurance.
- Rejuvenates and refreshes you by increasing your energy level.
- Assists in regulating hormones that cause sexual cravings.
- And can boost your confidence and self-love for your body.

Imagine a pill that —when taken in regular, healthy doses— can improve your physical health, your overall mood, and help you overcome sexual sin. Exercise is that pill! (Of course, drinking enough water, getting enough sleep, and eating a healthy diet helps too.) Picture how the benefits of regular exercise could aid you in your fight against lust, but don't stop there. Make this vision a reality by committing to a weekly exercise routine.

Since I am not a licensed physical trainer, I will leave the exercise recommendations to your doctor and other qualified health experts. However, I do want to leave you with one final, practical tip. Whatever you do, take it slowly, especially if you haven't been physically active for a while. Don't pressure yourself to be a marathon runner in week one. Instead, take it one step at a time and enjoy the journey to physical —and spiritual— fitness.

ROUTINES TO GET YOU STARTED

MORNING ROUTINE

- Wake up.
- Make your bed.
- Cleanse your face and brush your teeth.
- Spend time with God.
- Sit (in quiet or play something calming) as you delight in and acknowledge God's presence.
- Exercise.
- Shower and get dressed.
- Eat breakfast.
- Review your plans for the day.

BEDTIME ROUTINE

- Power down electronics an hour in advance.
- Prepare your outfit for tomorrow.
- Record your goals for tomorrow in your planner.
- Shower and dress down for bed.
- Spend time in silence, reflecting on the day's events and identifying times you *did*

ROUTINES TO GET YOU STARTED

and *did not* sense God's presence.
- Recall what you learned in your morning devotion.
- Journal your prayers.
- Sleep.

RETREAT ROUTINE

- Take a temporary break from social media to tune out any mental noise. Focus all of your attention on listening to God in scripture, silence, and prayer.

- Sit in stillness and quiet your thoughts as you acknowledge God's loving presence. Commit your day to Him and ask Him to give you a fresh experience of His love.
- Worship God through song and praise.
- Contemplate all that God has done for you and express your gratitude to Him.
- Go for a walk outside and look for God's beauty in nature.
- Read through a Bible plan (or listen to a sermon series or an audiobook) that speaks to your current spiritual needs.

- Journal your thoughts and anything that God impresses on your heart.
- Ask God to reveal any unconfessed sin you may have (and repent).

- Cast your anxieties on God and pray on behalf of others as well.
- Meditate on the gospel and reflect on the implications it has on your life.
- Sleep and rest.

come home.

RESET ROUTINE

- If possible, retreat to a place where you can freely pour out your heart to God without distractions or interruptions.

- Repent: Confess how you have specifically sinned against God. Acknowledge that your sin disrupts your relationship with God and, finally, express your desire to restore intimacy with Him.

- Believe and accept that you are forgiven: Take some time to meditate on the gospel. Remember that even in your sin, God loves you. still loves you. His love, grace, and forgiveness are sure. Let them lead you to repentance and a heart filled with Christ's gift of peace.

- Learn from your failure: In a journal, write down the circumstances that led up to this moral failure and consider at least three practical ways you could avoid repeating the same mistake.

- Confess and be accountable: Collaborate with your accountability partner. Bring your sin into the light, ask her for prayer, and discuss healthy, biblical ways to move forward from your relapse.

- Recommit yourself to pursuing biblical purity: Don't allow self-condemnation to stagnate your progress. Instead of viewing your failure, repentance, and recommitment to biblical purity as a setback, understand that as long as you recover, you're making forward progress in your walk with God.

CONNECT WITH TITANIA PAIGE

If you were inspired by *come home* and desire to deepen your relationship with Christ, I invite you to connect with me, Titania Paige. My passion is helping women release the shame and guilt of sexual impurity so they can receive the freedom, forgiveness, & healing offered in Christ.

I am the founder of the Purpose in Purity Podcast, available on Apple Podcasts, Stitcher, Spotify, and TuneIn. Join me for grace-filled conversations on surrendering our souls and sexuality to God.

Purpose in Purity exists to help Christian women navigate the spiritual journey from living a lifestyle of sexual sin to a lifestyle of complete satisfaction in Christ's love through:

Connect with Titania Paige

The Purpose in Purity Podcast
Show Notes and blog posts
Free membership in the Purpose in Purity Support Group
Books and resources

For more information about my ministry, visit www.TitaniaPaige.com.

To inquire about having me speak at your event, visit www.TitaniaPaige.com, and click on "speaking."

Instagram: @PurposeinPurityPodcast
Facebook: @TitaniaPaige
YouTube: Titania Paige

RECOMMENDED RESOURCES

BIBLICAL PURITY MINISTRIES

Adultery & Marital Affairs

AFFAIR RECOVERY: At Affair Recovery, we help people heal from the pain of affairs and betrayal. Our programs are research-based, combining a solid curriculum with the strength of collaborative support to provide solace and recovery for both couples and individuals. All of our materials are created by clinical professionals, all of whom have personally experienced infidelity. | AffairRecovery.com

KASEY VAN NORMAN: Kasey Van Norman is a professional counselor, Bible teacher, and the author of the books and study series, Named by God and Raw Faith. Kasey writes and teaches about the love that redeemed her life from the shame of past abuse, addiction, infidelity, and, strengthened her through a life-threatening cancer diagnosis. | KaseyVanNorman.com

recommended resources

Biblical Sexuality & Womanhood

AUTHENTIC INTIMACY: Authentic Intimacy is a unique teaching ministry devoted to teaching on God's design for intimacy and sexuality. | AuthenticIntimacy.com

GIRLDEFINED: Kristen Clark and Bethany Baird are sisters, lifelong friends, and the founders of GirlDefined Ministries. These Texas gals are passionate about God's beautiful design for womanhood and love sharing this message through blogging, speaking, and mentoring young women. | GirlDefined.com

Courtship & Engagement

WORTH THE WAIT: Worth the Wait is a relationship ministry created by Brandon and Sheretta Taylor. The couple started out in 2014 by documenting their time in courtship to offer practical advice from their experiences and to encourage others to have loving, purposeful relationships that honor and glorify God. Now married, they continue to share on the topic of relationships and marriage as the Lord leads them. Their primary desire is to see Christ lifted up and more Christian homes prepared for His soon coming. | Youtube.com/user/WorthTheWait518

Fornication & Singleness

THIS REDEEMED LIFE: This Redeemed Life was founded in 2007 as Redeemed Girl Ministries by Marian Jordan Ellis. Her story of how Jesus rescued her from a life of emptiness echoes through all we do at

come home.

TRL. Marian was an active Bible study teacher in her local church when she sensed the call to reach women who would normally never set foot in a church. Marian, a redeemed girl herself, is passionate that others experience the same life she discovered in Jesus Christ. | ThisRedeemedLife.org

TIFFANY DAWN: Tiffany is a 31-year-old speaker, author, & lover of coffee and beautiful things. She's also a woman who has battled an eating disorder and an awful dating relationship. For years, she hated herself, but she didn't want to tell anyone. She didn't think anyone would understand. | TiffanyDawn.net

NATALIE MET LEWIS: Natalie Met Lewis is the creator of The Devoted Life, a prompted journal for singles and author of Eternally Fixed, a bible study on cultivating an eternal perspective. She lives in Louisiana with her husband, Josh. | NatalieMetLewis.com

Homosexuality & Same-Sex Attraction

LIVING HOPE MINISTRIES: Living Hope Ministries is a Christian-based organization that supports men and women affected by same gender attraction through weekly support group meetings, mentoring, working with churches, and providing moderated online support forums for students, adults, and parents. | LiveHope.org

LONGING FOR INTIMACY: Longing for intimacy is a ministry that equips and encourages women who are struggling with pornography, wrestling with their sexuality, and for anyone looking to build deeper intimacy with Jesus. | LongingForIntimacy.com

RESTORED HOPE NETWORK: Restored Hope is a membership governed network dedicated to restoring hope to those broken by sexual and relational sin, especially those impacted by homosexuality. We proclaim that Jesus Christ has life-changing power for all who submit to Christ as Lord; we also seek to equip His church to impart that transformation. | RestoredHopeNetwork.org

Porn & Masturbation

JESSICA HARRIS: Jessica Harris is an author, blogger, international speaker and the creator of beggarsdaughter.com, a blog about the sexual struggles of women in the church and how they can find grace. | BeggarsDaughter.com

JOY SKARKA: Joy Skarka is passionate about creating spaces to free women from shame. It was in college that God saved Joy by his grace, and she began to experience freedom. Jesus healed Joy from the heartaches of sexual abuse and the pains of sexual addiction. Because of her story, she hopes to always write and speak authentically. | JoyPedrow.com

BOOKS

Gay Girl, Good God: The Story of Who I Was, and Who God Has Always Been, by Jackie Hill Perry | In *Gay Girl, Good God*, author Jackie Hill Perry shares her own story, offering practical tools that helped her in the process of finding wholeness. Jackie grew up fatherless and experienced gender confusion. She embraced masculinity and homosexuality with every fiber of her being. She knew that Christians had a lot to say about all of the above. But was she supposed to change herself? How was she supposed to stop loving women, when homosexuality felt more natural to her than heterosexuality ever could?

Hearing God: Developing a Conversational Relationship with God, by Dallas Willard | In this updated version of the classic, you'll gain rich spiritual insight into how we can hear God's voice clearly and develop an intimate partnership with him in the work of his kingdom. Including new material from Dallas Willard's teaching at the Renovaré Institute and reformatted to be even easier to read, this classic continues to endure as one of today's best resources for learning to listen closely to God.

Holy Sexuality and the Gospel: Sex, Desire, and Relationships Shaped by God's Grand Story, by Christopher Yuan | Dr. Christopher Yuan explores the concept of holy sexuality —chastity in singleness or faithfulness in marriage —in a practical and relevant manner, equipping readers with an accessible yet robust theology of sexuality. Whether you want to share Christ with a loved one who identifies as gay or you're wrestling with questions of identity yourself, this book will help you better understand sexuality in light of God's grand story and realize that holy sexuality is actually good news for all.

The Bondage Breaker®: Overcoming Negative

Thoughts, Irrational Feelings, & Habitual Sins, by Neil Anderson | Harmful habits, negative thinking, and irrational feelings can all lead to sinful behavior and keep you in bondage. If you feel trapped by any of these strongholds in your life, know that you are not alone—you *can* break free.

The Search for Significance: Seeing Your True Worth Through God's Eyes, by Robert McGee | Robert McGee's best-selling book has helped millions of readers learn how to be free to enjoy Christ's love while no longer basing their self-worth on their accomplishments or the opinions of others.

With: Reimagining the Way You Relate to God, by Skye Jethani | Who knew that a preposition had so much influence? Skye's book will challenge the way that you think about God and faith digging deep into our motivations and heart issues. You can't read this book and not see yourself and others differently!

CHRISTIAN ALBUMS

The Ruin, by Timothy Brindle | Birthed from a deep appreciation for the glory of God in the gospel of grace, timothy brindle has composed a collection of songs to encourage and admonish us to prize the gospel as precious.

The Atonement, by Shai Linne | The Atonement is a thematic lyrical presentation of the great saving work accomplished on the cross 2,000 years ago by Jesus Christ. Each song is an expression of either the neces-

come home.

sity of, the event of, or the implications of The Atonement.

The Attributes of God, by Shai Linne | "What comes into our minds when we think about God is the most important thing about us." -A.W. Tozer. As the title suggests, this is a concept album with the entire emphasis on the nature and character of God. Do you know Him?

ENTERTAINMENT CRITICS & FILTERS

MOVIEGUIDE: MOVIEGUIDE®'s mission is to redeem the values of the entertainment industry, according to biblical principles, by influencing industry executives and artists. | MovieGuide.org

COMMON SENSE MEDIA: Find age-appropriate movies, books, apps, TV shows, video games, websites, and music that you and your kids will love. Browse our library of more than 30,000 reviews by age, entertainment type, learning rating, genre, and more using the filters in the left column. | CommonSenseMedia.org

CLEARPLAY: Clearly helps make streaming movies family friendly. | Try.Clearplay.com

VIDANGEL: VidAngel provides a way to skip or mute things you don't want to see or hear in movies and TV shows. Want to skip the nudity in Game of Thrones? Go ahead. Don't like the mature language in Stranger Things? Mute it. Want less blood and gore in Hacksaw Ridge? VidAngel lets you skip and mute any objectionable content, all in the privacy of your home. | VidAngel.com

ENTERTAINMENT SUBSCRIPTIONS

FAITHLIFETV: Watch thousands of hours of edifying and entertaining movies, shows, and biblical teaching. | FaithLifeTV.com

PUREFLIX: Thousands of feel-good movies, inspirational documentaries, laugh-out-loud TV shows, and uplifting original content. | PureFlix.com

RIGHTNOW MEDIA: We provide Christians across the globe with resources that will inspire them to champion the mission Jesus gave to his people—making disciples of all nations. | RightNowMedia.org

UP FAITH & FAMILY: Make any room your family room with our uplifting, family-friendly streaming service. | UpFaithAndFamily.com

FILTERING SOFTWARE

COVENANT EYES: Our Accountability service helps you overcome porn by monitoring your screen activity and sending a report to a trusted ally who holds you accountable for your online choices. | By CovenantEyes.com

NETNANNY: Net Nanny uses modern content detection technology to look at every web page every time your kids click on a link, enter a URL or do search. | By NetNanny.com

VICTORY APP: The fight for freedom from pornography is a battle you can win. But, every battle needs a plan. The Victory app provides a strategic battle plan come home. for liberty in the struggle against pornography. | By TheVictoryApp.com

PODCASTS

JAVA WITH JULI: Java with Juli is a fresh, relevant, and conversational new podcast wrestling with questions about relationships and sexuality. | AuthenticIntimacy.com/Podcast

PURITY FOR LIFE: Purity for Life is the weekly podcast from Pure Life Ministries. Each episode will take you where real life meets real Christianity as we tackle the tough issues for those struggling with sexual sin. | PureLifeMinistries.org

PROFESSIONAL CHRISTIAN COUNSELING

CHRISTIAN CARE CONNECT: Find the right Christian Counselors, Coaches and Clinics for your needs with their searchable directory. | Connect.AACC.net

CHRISTIAN COUNSELOR NETWORK: *Focus on The Family* can help you bring healing and restoration to your family with Christian perspectives you can trust by connecting you with licensed Christian counselors in your area. | FocusOnTheFamily.com/Get-Help/Counseling-Services-and-Referrals

CRYSTAL RENAUD DAY: Crystal Renaud Day, MAPC is a pastoral counselor, life coach, speaker, and author based in Kansas City. With over a decade of ministry experience, she works with women, couples, and teen girls on a variety of emotional and relational issues. | LivingOnPurposeKC.com

FACEBOOK SUPPORT GROUPS

SHERECOVERY: SheRecovery Virtual Recovery Meetings hosted by Crystal Renaud Day, MAPC. These weekly meetings are designed to provide women who struggle with addiction with accountability, recovery tools, spiritual growth, prayer, and more. Women are encouraged to attend each week, seek an accountability partner at the meetings to connect with day to day, and join the SheRecovery Online Community for further support. | LivingOnPurposeKC.com/SheRecovery

REFERENCES

Allen, J. (2020). *Get out of your head: Stopping the spiral of toxic thoughts.* Colorado Springs, CO: Waterbrook.

Douglas, J.D & Tenney, M. C. (Eds). (1987). *Zondervan illustrated bible dictionary.* Grand Rapids, MI: Zondervan.

How porn affects the brain like a drug. (2017, August 23). Retrieved from https://fightthenewdrug.org/how-porn-affects-the-brain-like-a-drug/

McGee, R.S. (1998). *The search for significance: Seeing your true worth through God's eyes.* Nashville, TN: W Publishing Group, Thomas Nelson.

Perry, J. H. (2018*). Gay girl, good god: The story of who I was, and who God has always been.* Nashville, TN: B&H Publishing Group.

Piper, J. (2019, November 21). Do I need to hear from God before I make a decision [Podcast] Retrieved from https://www.desiringgod.org/interviews/do-i-need-to-hear-from-God-before-i-make-a-decision

Piper, J. (2020, June 11). How should I handle my regrets? [Podcast] Retrieved from https://www.

desiringGod.org/interviews/how-should-i-handle-my-regrets

Should a Christian exercise? (n.d.). Retrieved June 14, 2020, from https://www.gotquestions.org/Christian-exercise.html

Sun Tzu. (2019). *The art of war.* United States: Dover Publications.

Waltke, B. "Heart." (n.d.). Retrieved on March 28, 2020 from https://www.biblestudytools.com/dictionary/heart/

What does the bible say about being stiff-necked? (n.d.). Retrieved from https://www.gotquestions.org/Bible-stiff-necked.html

What is companion planting? (n.d.). Retrieved from https://www.gardenista.com/posts/garden-decoder-what-is-companion-planting-gardening-best-vegetable-companions/

Who is Satan? (n.d.). Retrieved from https://www.gotquestions.org/who-Satan.html

Willard, D. (2012). *Hearing God: Developing a conversational relationship with God.* Downers Grove, IL: InterVarsity Press.

ACKNOWLEDGMENTS

If you're reading this, it means you cared enough to see me arrive at this mountaintop called "writing a book." It's been mighty cold out here on these book-writing-slopes, and I seriously under-estimated how mentally fatiguing this climb would be. There were times I'd gain so much ground in going the traditionally-published-book-route, only to be knocked back down by circumstances beyond my control. If it were not for God's grace, this manuscript would have been suspended in limbo while I yo-yoed between my triumphs and my disappointments. Thanks to many amazing people God used in my life, I was able to see this assignment through to the end via self-publishing. So I'd like to take this time to thank everyone who helped me reach the peak of this beautiful yet challenging journey.

To My Husband:
Without your love and firm support, I'm not confident that I could have dared to dream that God could use my writing. You have always been a pillar in my life and ministry. Sometimes, I forget that I am leaning on you. Your faithful love and reliability have taught me to be secure enough to stretch out my hand to reach

toward all that God calls me to be. You are forever the love of my life and my most significant source of encouragement.

To Gabrielle:

I love you. You are a treasure that I long to keep precious and safe. I pray that by leaving this spiritual legacy to you in this book (and my own life), that you won't make the same mistakes I did. But also, I want to assure you of God's great power to use the mistakes you will make for His glory and your good. (Romans 8:28) You are altogether beautiful, my daughter.

To My Family:

Thank you, Venus Brown (aka "Mommy"), for loving me and believing in me as both your child and your friend. You are truly legendary, and you are an irreplaceable figure in my world. Thank you, Momma Vicki, for being an example of grace, goofy-charm, and resilience in the face of life's boogeymen. Thank you, Dorrian and Mitchell, for teaching me to be a better communicator of God's love in every aspect of my character. Talor, you are my spirit-animal, infused with sarcasm and nerdy wit. Without you all in my corner, I would not have grown into the woman who finished this book.

To My Church:

Thank you, River Community Church of Cookeville, TN. You welcomed me into God's family and invested in me when I didn't see my worth and potential in Christ. To the Tiebout Family, the Cook family, the

come home.

Thorpe family, and all of my besties that grew up with me in the faith at The Gathering College Ministry, you are all lights on a hill to me.

Thank you, Unashamed Church Memphis, for your unwavering love and support of me. Thank you for encouraging me to use my gifts and for every prayer and financial investment you made to demonstrate it. I praise God for the excellent leadership of Pastor Charles Cotton, our former Pastor Dr. Mondonico Williams, along with our elders, David Rogers and John Mack. I love you all like flesh and blood.

To the Purpose in Purity Community:

Without your presence and engagement in my life, quitting would have been a piece of cake. Meeting each of you has satisfied my need to see the women my ministry touches. You'll never know how much the privilege of being in your life, and watching you grow spiritually has affected me. As Paul wrote to the Philippians, "you are my joy and the crown I receive for my work" (Philippians 4:1).

To My Crowd-Funding Support:

Thanks to the generosity of the following financial supporters, money was not a source of anxiety for me as I finished this book. Thank you so much for believing in my ministry and the message of this book. Thank you to:

Abby Grigsby
Antoinette Dupree
Ashley Yates
Brittany Robinson

Casey Grooms
Christina Patterson of
    BelovedWomen.org
Ciera Aguer

Claudine Thompson
Dana Arnold of The Hope Collective
Dorrian Kerlegan
Folakemi Awe
Janice Fitzhugh
Jen Dunnewold of MyHeartFireStudio (Etsy)
Kayli Minami
Kendra Tillman of StrongHer.Me
LaWanna Wilson
Melissa Davis
Rachel Cotton
Talor Paige
Tammara Houston
The Cook Family
Tiarna Pertovt

Book Credits:

Thank you to the Proverbs 31 Ministries' First 5 editing team and the CompelTraining.com team, who have been instrumental in my growth as a writer.

Thank you to Beatrice from BeatriceViyiwi.Etsy.com for supplying me with beautiful handmade florals (as seen in my logo).

Thank you to Amy and Melanie of NextStepCoachingServices.com, for providing an enjoyable editing experience from start to finish.

Thank you to my designers from 99Designs.com. Anastasia S., you made the cover of my book a masterpiece. RosannaWhiteDesigns, you brought my vision for the book interior to life! Thank you, both.

Keep journaling through your journey to a lifestyle of biblical purity with these free BONUS exercises and prompts.

FREE WORKSHEETS

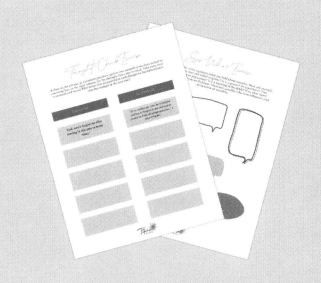

TitaniaPaige.com

Made in the USA
Middletown, DE
18 July 2020